The Shopkeeper's Handbook

Other Titles in the Better Business Series

How to Start and Run Your Own Business, 7th edition 1989, M. Mogano

How to Start and Run Your Own Shop, 2nd edition 1988, P. Levene

How to Give a Successful Presentation, 1988, I. Richards

Forthcoming title

How to Get a Better Job, 1989, M. Mogano

Cover shows the NCR 2127 programmable EPOS terminal, one of a range of EPOS terminals developed by NCR for retailers' specific requirements. For further information: 01-725 8474.

Better Business Series

The Shopkeeper's Handbook

P. Levene

Graham & Trotman
A member of the Kluwer Academic Publishers Group
LONDON/DORDRECHT/BOSTON

First published in 1989 by

Graham & Trotman Limited
Sterling House
66 Wilton Road
London SW1V 1DE
UK

Graham & Trotman Inc.
Kluwer Academic Publishers Group
101 Philip Drive
Assinippi Park
Norwell, MA 02061
USA

© P. Levene, 1989

British Library Cataloguing in Publication Data

Levene, P. (Peter)
 The shopkeeper's handbook
 1. Shopkeeping manuals
 I. Title   II. Series
 658.8'7

 ISBN 1-853331-70-8
 ISBN 1-853331-71-6 Pbk
 ISBN 1-853330-88-4 Series

Library of Congress Cataloging-in-Publication Data

Levene, P. (Peter)
 The shopkeeper's handbook.

 (Better business series)
 Includes index.
 1. Stores, Retail—Management.   2. Retail trade—
Management.   I. Title.   II. Series.
HF5429.L482   1989   658.8'7   88-29659
ISBN 1-85333-170-8
ISBN 1-85333-171-6 (pbk.)

This publication is protected by International Copyright Law. All rights reserved. No part of this publication may be reproduced, stored in a retrieval system, or transmitted in any form or by any means, electronic, mechanical, photocopying, recording or otherwise, without the prior permission of the copyright holder.

Typeset in Garamond by Colset Private Ltd, Singapore
Printed and bound in Great Britain by
Billing & Sons Ltd, Worcester

Contents

	PREFACE	vii
Chapter 1	THE SHOP AND EQUIPMENT Appearances • Cleaning and Hygiene • Floor Space • Equipment • Saving Money • Fire Precautions •	1
Chapter 2	STOCK RANGE AND MERCHANDISING Profit • Stockroom • Stock • Promotions and Pricing • Add New Lines •	15
Chapter 3	REPS AND DELIVERY MEN Sales Representatives • Deliveries •	33
Chapter 4	CUSTOMER RELATIONS Selling to the Customer • Customer Complaints • The Customer and Money • Asking Customer to Do Things •	36
Chapter 5	POPULAR TRADES Grocers • **Delicatessens and Delicatessen Counters:** Dairy Facts • Cheese • Meat • Vacuum Packing • Cutting • Cleaning and Hygiene • Increase Sales • **Bacon:** Cutting • Ways to Sell • **In Store Bakeries:** Cost • What You Need • Method • Extra Impulse Sales • **Fast Foods:** 'Fast' Foods • **Microwaves** • **Greengrocers:** Fruit and Vegetables • Self Selection • **Newsagents:** Canvassing for New Customers • Paperboys and Papergirls • Increase Profit • **Video Rental:** The Future of Videos • Questions to Ask • **Off Licences:** Applying for a Licence • The Law • Alcohol by	42

Volume/Original Gravity/Proof • Displaying Wines • Christmas Insurance •

| Chapter 6 | **REFRIGERATION** | 72 |

Freezer Displays • Freezing Food • Maintenance of Freezers • Chilled Cabinets •

| Chapter 7 | **STAFF** | 80 |

Engaging Staff • Staff Management • Wages • Security • Educating Your Staff •

| Chapter 8 | **SECURITY** | 86 |

Cheques • Tills • Shoplifting • Deterrents • Credit Information Agencies • Small Claims Fees • Shop Premises • Deterrents • Handling Cash •

| Chapter 9 | **BOOKWORK** | 99 |

Stocktaking • Banking • Insurance • Pensions • Account Books • Tax • General Bookwork •

| Chapter 10 | **BUYING AND SELLING A SHOP** | 120 |

Selling Buying •

| Chapter 11 | **THE LAW AND THE SHOPKEEPER** | 126 |

The Shopkeeper • Personnel • The Customer •

| Chapter 12 | **REFERENCE SECTION** | 145 |

INDEX 154

Preface

In *How to Start and Run Your Own Shop* I dealt with the basics of selecting, buying, and running a shop, and also included the main points of legislation that affect shopkeepers. This book, *The Shopkeeper's Handbook*, is the logical sequel and deals with the 'nuts and bolts' of everyday shop life. The two books together not only provide a complete insight into owning a shop, but also serve as a most useful reference manual.

The main aim of *The Shopkeeper's Handbook* is to help with problems, give guidelines for new situations, and to spur the imagination into creating more profit and pleasure from your business.

In order to receive the most benefit from the book, it is suggested that when you read a passage that could be of use to you, or something that could be adapted to fit a different situation, you immediately make a note of it, lest you forget.

As far as layout is concerned, I have tried to group facts together as far as possible, but because shop life is so intermingled it is impossible to make clear-cut divisions.

Lastly, the word 'he' has been used throughout the book purely for consistency and should not on any account be taken as an indication of sex discrimination!

CHAPTER 1

The Shop and Equipment

'Don't spoil the ship for a ha'p'orth of tar.'

Appearances

See Your Shop in its True Light

Do you know what your shop really looks like both from the inside and the outside? This may seem a very strange question, but give it some thought, especially if you have been there for some time, and try to see it from the viewpoint of someone who has just moved into the neighbourhood. The point of the matter is, would the outside of your shop encourage a potential customer to come in, and if so, what would be his first impressions? It is amazing the number of shopkeepers who never ever take the time to look at the outside of their shop properly and see it in its true light.

Shopfronts

If the woodwork in your shopfront shows signs of deterioration, you have several options:

(1) You can have the old wood cut out and replaced. This is the cheapest method and not necessarily the worst.
(2) You can have a new metal shopfront.
(3) You can have only the existing glass, wooden frame, and door replaced. Local carpenters will be able to quote for this, and planning permission will not be necessary. Obtain quotes for each method before deciding. (See also 'Planning Permission' page 2.)

Estimates and quotations   If you ask for a price for work you want done, it is important that you realise the difference between an estimate and a quotation. An estimate is really a professional guess—the final amount payable may be more or less depending on the actual amount of work that is necessary to be done. A quotation, on the other hand, is an actual figure for doing the job. Once you accept this figure you will have entered into a binding contract for the contractors to do the work described and you to pay the amount of money agreed. The two terms are quite often used very loosely, so you should always make sure each party knows exactly what is meant, and whether or not the figure mentioned includes VAT.

Planning permission   Certain alterations to your shopfront will need planning permission, even replacing an old wooden one with a new aluminium design needs it. So, if you are thinking of changing anything, contact your local planning office before spending any money.

Landlord's permission   If you are a leaseholder you will also have to obtain the permission of the landlord. This is usually no problem if it improves the property.

Improvements   Improvements to properties which have been carried out by the tenant with the landlord's permission cannot be considered when a new rent is being determined, unless the improvement is part of a condition of the lease.

Shutters and Windows

One of the added benefits of having shutters fitted is the fact that because your windows will be covered over for half of each day, they will stay cleaner twice as long. This means that if your window cleaner were to call half as often, it is possible you could recover the cost of the shutters in about 20 years through savings made on window cleaning! Alternatively, you could carry on as you do, but have your windows looking twice as bright.

Metal shutters   If, because of vandalism, you decide to invest in metal shutters on your shopfront, get several quotes and compare specifications as well as prices. It is good sense to introduce yourself into any shop that has had shutters fitted recently to find out who installed them, whether the shopkeeper is satisfied with them, and, if he does not mind answering, how much they cost.

If you have shutters installed with padlocks, the *first* thing you must do is place one of the keys on your keyring, so that when you try it out you do not lock yourself out of the shop!

Shutters and break-ins   A disadvantage of shutters is that if anyone breaks in from the rear of the premises they will not be seen in the shop from the street. You must, therefore, take a fresh look at your security arrangements at the rear of the building and reinforce wherever necessary. (See Chapter 8.)

THE SHOP AND EQUIPMENT

Receipts for Work Done

If you are paying cash for work done by a person or company and you feel uncertain about whether or not you will receive a proper receipt, be prepared and write or type out your own on the following lines, and get them to sign it before leaving.

1 January 1988
Cost of supplying and fitting metal shutters to all shop windows and door of 'The Candy Box' 1285 Little Lane, Bigshot £1,500.00
Deposit Paid 500.00
Balance £1,000.00
Received on behalf of The Metal Shutter Co., Bigg Lane, Littleshot, the sum of £1,000.00 cash.

SIGNED ....

Coat of Paint Outside

A fresh coat of paint on the outside of the shop only costs a few pounds and may encourage newcomers to the area to try the shop. Once inside, of course, they will be made into regulars by your friendliness and charm! Keeping the shopfront clean and bright is probably one of the cheapest and best methods of advertising available to you.

Front Door Open

Keep your front door open for as long as possible (weather permitting). This is much more inviting to passers-by. If he has the choice of making his purchase in more than one shop, the customer, being basically lazy, will choose the one where he can enter with the least effort.

Cold outside, warm inside When the weather is cold outside, try to keep your shop warm so that customers are encouraged to stay a little longer and, hopefully, spend more.

Minimum temperatures There is no minimum working temperature as far as shops which are open to the public are concerned, although staff should be allowed to warm themselves now and again. The minimum temperatures referred to in law apply only to premises where the public do not have access.

Flooring

Possibly the most striking thing about a shop, once you have entered it, is the floor. Just as a new fitted carpet can completely alter the visual impact of a room, so can the condition of your lino or tiles set the tone of your shop. If your floor is worn out in places and you cannot afford to have it all renewed, make sure you repair the parts that are unsightly. If you cannot do it yourself, ask a flooring firm to have a look and make some suggestions.

Painted Walls

Take a look at your walls—the parts that are showing, that is. Do they need a coat of paint? This can be done for a minimal cost, takes no time at all, and can vastly improve the image of the shop.

Ceilings

When was the last time your ceiling was painted? It is highly probable that even if there are no stain marks, it will be nicotine brown in colour! You may paint the ceiling whatever colour you like, but remember, the lighter the shade the more effective it will be for reflecting light back into your shop.

Painting The easiest and fastest way of actually painting a ceiling is by using a roller on the end of a broom handle. One of the many textured coatings on the market may be useful if the ceiling is badly cracked.

Stain marks Paint over unsightly stain marks with undercoat, not emulsion.

Suspended ceilings You could also contact a firm to give an estimate for installing a new suspended ceiling. This is particularly beneficial if the existing ceiling is very high. But remember if you do this, you will also have to alter your lighting. If you do have a suspended ceiling fitted, you will find it an ideal medium for hiding cables for power or security cameras in various parts of the shop.

Modern lighting Of course, if you are thinking of modernising your lighting, why not do it in conjunction with a new suspended ceiling? You will probably find that part of the cost of the ceiling can be subsidised by the saving on the electrical side.

Lighting

Do not try to economise by turning off some of the shop lights, or by failing to replace dead fluorescent tubes. Lighting is a relatively low-priced expense, and should not be cut back on. Do not forget that customers come into your shop to *see* what you have for sale!

Strip lighting Strip lighting in the shop as well as spot lights can enhance wall shelving and special displays when strategically placed. Take a look around and see if you have any dull spots.

THE SHOP AND EQUIPMENT

Wipe over lights Wipe over lights periodically to get the full benefit from them. A quarter of an inch dust filter can cut down the light considerably.

Fluorescent tubes Keep an eye on fluorescent tubes because they gradually grow dimmer over a period of time. This is why some shops make a practice of changing all the tubes at set intervals, rather than waiting for them to burn out. It saves time and trouble if you always keep a spare fluorescent tube for emergencies. Ideally, you should have one of each size and type used—not only for ceiling lighting but also for display cabinets and insect electrocutors. This way you will not be stuck if an important light gives up the ghost at an awkward time, such as when you are very busy or at a weekend or Bank Holiday.

Shelves

You can give the impression of having new shelving simply by replacing the front plastic edging strips with a bright new colour. After all, when the shelves are filled, this is the only part the customer can see! Old shelving can be modernised by buying front edging strips with inserts as above, and fixing them to the front of the shelves.

Music

Some people find background music in a shop relaxing, others disconcerting. If you contemplate installing a music system in your shop, do not forget that you will have to be licensed by the Performing Rights Society.

Christmas Decorations

If you decorate your shop at Christmas time, you can save money and prepare for the next year by taking stock of your decorations before you take them down after Christmas, and by looking around for half-price offers.

If you are going to decorate your shop, do it properly. A couple of garlands here and there look pathetic.

Cats and Dogs

Don't allow your own cats and dogs into the shop. If you do you will find that some customers will stay away because they think animals are unhygienic, others will stay away because they are scared.

Fix some rings outside the shop for owners to tie up their dogs, but do not place them too close together or you may end up with a dog fight!

Notice Boards

People are always interested in reading notices, and a notice board will attract potential customers to your shop. You can place notices on your shop door, window, or somewhere inside your shop. There are two ways of running it.

(1) Take in notices free of charge for a certain length of time until the allocated space is filled, then use a 'first in/first out' basis. This will ensure that you get plenty of advertisements and plenty of customers to look.
(2) Charge a certain amount per week, say 20p. Write the expiry date on the back of the card. To encourage people to use the board, leave a substantial number on display all of the time.

'A' Boards

If you have a large enough forecourt, make use of 'A' boards to advertise special offers or topical/seasonal lines. These are far more effective than window posters. If you are in a country area try to position them so that motorists will see the board before they reach the shop, even if it means using a grass verge or piece of wasteland.

Posters and Signs

If you are writing your own posters for the window, or signs for inside the shop, keep the lettering simple and do not make spelling mistakes. Unless you have studied calligraphy, do not try any fancy lettering.

Local Events

Keep an eye open for local events where you can promote or supply your goods.

Cleaning and Hygiene

Glass

It may seem obvious, but the best way to clean glass in serve-overs etc., is with plenty of hot water, and then to polish with a piece of kitchen towel. If you use glass or furniture polish, or an all-purpose cleaner, you may leave an odour which is fine in your house, but which will not encourage your customers to buy your ham.

Equipment

Equipment used for fresh food, such as scales and slicers, should be cleaned frequently and at least once a day thoroughly.

THE SHOP AND EQUIPMENT

Slicers Never use a knife for cleaning the blade of a slicing machine. Admittedly it does remove any build up efficiently, but it will also make tiny scratch marks on the surface of the blade which will eventually rust, and not prove very popular with the Health Inspector; and new blades are not cheap.

Soak

When washing down slicers, counters, etc., do not waste time continually rubbing at the same spot to get it clean. Instead, cover with a liberal amount of hot water and carry on doing something else whilst it soaks. When you come back, it will only take a fraction of the time to finish.

Health Regulations

The health regulations require that you use different knives, spatulas, tongs etc. for handling uncooked meat and bacon to those that you use for cooked meats and other ready-to-eat foods.

Bottles and Crates

Returnable empty bottles and crates take up a lot of room if stored indoors, and are a temptation for youngsters to steal if they are left outside. Not only is it much easier to sell non-returnable bottles, but it ties up less money, and saves having to check that the delivery men have taken the correct number and given sufficient credit.

Bulk Waste Containers

Do you have a bulk waste container and if so are you making the best use of it? Do you have arguments with the dustmen about boxes of cardboard that will not fit in, and which they say they are not supposed to clear? You can alleviate the problems to a degree by following this method of filling a container. First of all, never put in whole boxes. Always break them down and lay them flat in the container. Have a large piece of wood handy and tamp the rubbish down every foot or so. Standing on a upturned crate helps. Push the cardboard down the sides, and when you reach the top of the container make it taller by wedging large pieces of cardboard all the way round. Do not concern yourself with the fact that it may be difficult for the dustmen to empty—that is their job.

Floor Space

Traffic Jams

Watch the traffic flow in your shop to see if you have any hold-ups, and either rearrange fixtures or goods to keep the traffic flowing. Most customers cannot be bothered to queue or wait for what they want and some sales will be lost if this is the case.

Height of Gondolas

Different people have differing views on how high central gondola shelving should be. Everyone agrees that as far as shelving footage is concerned, the higher the better. The argument revolves around security of stock, in other words—shoplifting. Make up your own mind after reading both sides of the argument.

Low Gondolas
FOR: You can see exactly who is in the shop, and where they are.
AGAINST: If you can see them, they can see you. They will know exactly where all the staff are all the time, and even though the gondolas are low, they are not low enough to see where the customer's hands are.

Tall Gondolas
FOR: More stock is able to be displayed. There is also a certain amount of risk to the potential thief, because he will not know where anyone is in the shop, and will realise he could be unexpectedly disturbed at any time, by someone turning the corner.
AGAINST: You cannot see who is in the shop, BUT with cameras from a closed circuit TV system positioned strategically, you will be able to watch them without being seen yourself.

Fans

If you have extractor fans in your shop, make sure staff keep the space around and in front of them clear and not blocked with piles of stock.

Making decisions Do you find it easy making decisions? Serious ones, that is. All too often the real issues become obscured because too much emphasis is placed on minor items or those full of sentimentality.

One method of aiding decision making is to take a sheet of paper, draw a line vertically down the centre, head one side 'FOR' and the other 'AGAINST'. List everything you can think of on the relevant side, and you will then see the whole thing in perspective. It is amazing how much clearer everything becomes once it is written down.

Shop Too Large for Trade

Consider letting part of your shop if the trade does not warrant the square footage. I know that whatever sized shop we have, we could always do with more, but if your shop is large enough and you think you could take the same money from a smaller area, why not do so? All you need is to find someone who will not be competing with your own trade. As an example, estate agents are mushrooming all over the country and do not need huge premises, nor do building societies.

Equipment

Buying

Shop around when buying expensive equipment. Compare materials, size, and general specifications. Buy the correct equipment for your needs, in other words do not cut back, and do not waste money buying something larger than you need.

Service Contracts

When buying equipment for your shop try to buy from local firms, and find out the callout charges from various companies before deciding whether or not to take out a service contract. Everyone's circumstances differ, of course, but it is fairly safe to assume that taken over a number of years savings can be made by not having service contracts.

Look Ahead When Purchasing Equipment

Try to look ahead with regard to renewing equipment. For example, if you think a fridge or freezer is nearing the end of its life, it would be better to buy another in the winter, when various discounts may be had, than to wait until it packs up in the hot summer, and you then have to take your place in the queue with all the other shopkeepers crying out for service and new freezers.

Will It Go Through the Door?

Check the width of your door before ordering large pieces of equipment. Remember that you can usually gain an inch or two if you remove the door from its frame. If it will not go through the door, obtain a quote for removing the window etc. *before* making up your mind.

Unknown Makes of Equipment

If the piece of equipment you are thinking of buying is not a name you know, ask for the names and addresses of a few shops that have already bought it. Then phone them up, ask for their comments, and, if possible, go round to see what the piece of equipment looks like after it has been used for a little while.

Spare Parts

Ask how long the model has been produced, how much longer it will be produced, and how easy spares are to obtain. Although you should never accept the rep's word as gospel, you should get some idea as to its future availability.

Secondhand—Nameplates

If the equipment is secondhand, make sure it has a manufacturer's nameplate so that if repairs are needed, the make and model number can easily be found.

Reconditioned Equipment

If you buy reconditioned equipment make sure you get a guarantee.

Spare Cash Register and Scale

It is a good idea to keep an eye open for a cheap secondhand cash register and scale for emergency use. It does not matter how good your present service agreement is, even a couple of hours is a long time to wait with nothing working, especially when you consider that whenever anything goes wrong in the shop it is always subject to 'Sod's Law' i.e. evenings, weekends, and Bank Holidays. There is another advantage in buying a cheap secondhand mechanical till or scale for back-up use and that is in the event of a power cut or failure you will be able to carry on with your business, providing there is enough light, of course.

Guarantees

Before deciding on that new piece of equipment find out exactly what is covered by the guarantee and for how long.

Make sure you read the instruction manual thoroughly for any new equipment you purchase, and carry out any routine maintenance suggested. If you do not, and something goes wrong, it could invalidate the guarantee and you may be faced with a very large bill.

Delivery and Installation

Find out also whether the price includes the cost of delivery and installation, or whether these are 'additional extras'.

Inspect Before Signing for Equipment

Do not accept or sign for any equipment until you have had time to inspect it and to make sure it is working correctly. Never mind if the delivery man or rep becomes impatient—you are doing him a favour by buying his product, he is not doing you one.

Continuity

Some companies are more interested in selling the equipment than they are in the product that goes inside. Some are more interested in supplying you with the product. Make sure that whatever you buy, there is a regular supply and delivery service for it.

Paying for It

Having decided on the model give yourself plenty of time to weigh up all the pros and cons of paying for it in different ways. Your accountant should be able to help.

Cash Versus Lease or Hire Purchase

It is very tempting to take out lease agreements or hire purchase to replace an existing piece of equipment, but the repayments can act as millstones round your neck for years. It is much better for your peace of mind to save up sufficient money and then buy it outright taking advantage of all available discounts. If you think that you will never be able to save sufficient, how do you think you will repay it? It is a very rare occurrence indeed when a new piece of equipment generates enough *extra* sales to pay for itself.

Nominal Charges

If the equipment is going to be your property at the end of a primary leasing/renting period, make sure you have, in writing, the nominal charge which will be made.

Leasing Agreements

Make sure you understand every word printed on an agreement and the implications before signing any document. If you are not absolutely certain ask for a couple of days to think it over and get advice. Apart from asking a solicitor to look at it for you, you could also take the agreement along to your local Trading Standards Office for its comments.

Contract is Legally Binding

Remember that a contract is legally binding, and once you have signed it you have agreed to *everything* that is written within it. It does not matter what a rep says, if it is not written down, forget it.

Leasing/Hire Purchase

Find out exactly what you are getting when you are offered terms on equipment you are buying. Leasing, leasehire, lease purchase etc., are all terms that can be very ambiguous. Find out how much you have to pay, how long you will have to pay it for, and who will own the equipment at the end of the period.

Moving Shop Equipment

To avoid damaging yourself when altering the position of heavy shop fittings or equipment, particularly refrigeration, make use of rollers. Two broom handles would do if necessary, but short lengths of scaffolding poles are ideal, because they are obviously far stronger. All you need to do is lift one end of the freezer etc. sufficiently to slide a pole underneath, and then roll the equipment forward until you reach the point of balance, then slip the other pole under and carry on. You will find that using this method you will also be able to virtually turn the equipment on a sixpence (for those not old enough to remember sixpences, substitute a penny).

Saving Money

Payphones

It does not matter even if you have a public telephone box outside your shop, you can still make good profits and provide a service to the public by installing a payphone. These can be purchased very reasonably nowadays and can be programmed to provide whatever level of return you desire.

Letting Customers Use Your Telephone

If you do not have a payphone, you should be aware of the cost to you per telephone call, and then make an appropriate charge if you allow a customer to use it. For instance, a local telephone call made before one o'clock in the afternoon will cost you a fraction over 5p per minute. Therefore, if a customer makes a four minute call and gives you 10p, you will actually be PAYING HIM 10p for using your telephone.

Water Meters

Most shops use only a minimal amount of water—usually just a WC and two or three sinks. A tremendous amount of money can be saved by having a water meter installed and only paying for what you use. There is an initial installation cost plus standing charges, but even so, compared to paying your water rates based on the rateable value of the property you should still save hundreds of pounds in the first year, and more still in the following years.

Saving Electricity

To save on electricity costs, everything that does not need to be switched on should be switched off when closing at night. This usually just leaves the refrigeration. The following morning do not automatically switch on an appliance if it will not be needed until later. This is particularly important in the summer months when any extra heat put into the shop will make the

THE SHOP AND EQUIPMENT 13

refrigeration units work that much harder. For example, heat sealers can be left in the 'off' position until needed because they only take a couple of seconds to heat up.

Customer's Receipts

More savings can be made by turning off the customer receipt in the till. Ninety nine per cent of these pieces of paper end up left on the counter or the floor and are nothing but a nuisance. You will soon get to know which customers require a receipt, and it is no problem switching the button just for them.

Use Other Side of Till Rolls

Whenever you reduce your expenses, you increase your profit by the same amount. One area where it is possible to make cuts without losing efficiency is with the underside of till rolls in the cash register. Once the roll has been used, reverse it and utilise the other side. This will automatically halve the cost of these rolls!

First Loss, Best Loss

'Your first loss is your best loss'. This old adage was told to me many years ago by someone who had spent all his life in the grocery trade, and it is still as true today as it was when he first heard it. For example, say you have goods which have just gone out of date or are showing signs of deterioration. You should reduce them by a sufficient amount to ensure they all sell quickly. If you do not reduce them, or do so by only a penny or two, you will find that they eventually reach such a stage that they will have to be thrown away, and you will not get any of your money back.

Shop Hours

Study how many people pass your shop on different days and at different times, and adjust your opening hours to suit.

Fire Precautions

Statistics

Fire can destroy your property, your personal belongings, your livelihood, and the lives of anyone who happens to be in the shop. Do not think that it cannot happen to you. It can. In 1981 fire brigades were called out to just under 4,300 retail premises. Of these, almost a third were started by smokers' materials or electrical wiring and lighting. These figures are typical of most years.

Eighty per cent of fires occur when shops are closed. Surprised? If you and your family live above the shop, it's just plain commonsense to be extra vigilant at all times.

Smoking

Do not smoke in the shop or allow the staff to do so. Bear in mind that an increasing number of customers dislike the smell of cigarette smoke intensely. If you must smoke, make sure all ashtrays and waste paper bins are emptied daily, and not left overnight.

Cigarette Ends and Cardboard

If you keep waste rubbish and cardboard outside the back of the shop, bear in mind the possibility of a lighted cigarette end being thrown over a fence or wall and causing a fire.

Electric Cables

Make sure you do not have any trailing electric wires, especially near fridges and freezers, and if you have any joins in the cable they should be properly made and fixed above floor level so that water cannot penetrate.

Fire Extinguishers

Have the correct type of fire extinguisher and/or fire blanket for your goods and premises handy, particularly near storage areas, and ensure all members of staff know how to use them. The drawback to most of these extinguishers is their weight, which is usually too heavy for a woman assistant to handle effectively. It is a good idea therefore, to keep in addition to your normal extinguisher, a small gas filled multi-purpose one on the wall, which anyone can use, and which will deal very effectively with most small outbreaks if caught quickly enough.

Security Walk

Check carefully around the shop every evening after closing time. This is a security walk. It's not only to check that all doors and windows are properly locked and that any non-essential electrical equipment is switched off, but also to look for potential dangers of any kind.

Insurance and Advice

To have peace of mind, make sure you are fully insured against fire. Free advice on fire prevention may be obtained by asking your local Fire Prevention Officer to look over your premises.

CHAPTER 2

Stock range and Merchandising

'Where there's a will there's a way.'

Profit

Profit Margins

Be perfectly clear in your mind as to exactly what is meant by 'gross profit margin', or 'percentage of profit'. The profit margin you speak of is profit on return (POR), that is the amount of profit you earn on the selling price. There is a very simple method of working this out. All you need do is imagine the selling price of an article is 100 per cent of the price.

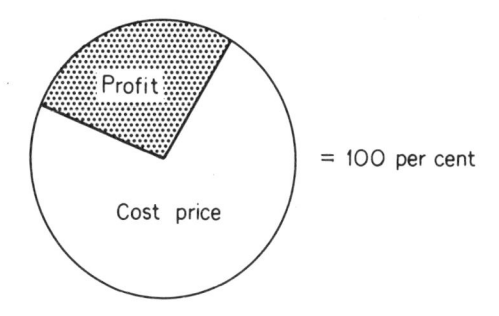

(Diagram: circle divided into 'Profit' and 'Cost price' segments = 100 per cent)

Therefore, if you wish to earn for example 32 per cent profit, the cost price must equal 68 per cent (100 − 32). If you want to earn 16.25 per cent, the cost price equals 83.75 per cent. If you want to earn 60 per cent, the cost equals 40 per cent. Once you know what the cost figure is equal to, just divide by the cost percentage number and multiply by 100 to obtain the selling price. Working out the above examples at a unit cost price of 77p, you have:

(1) (32 per cent) .77/68 × 100 = £1.13
(2) (16¼ per cent) .77/83.75 × 100 = 92p
(3) (60 per cent) .77/40 × 100 = £1.93

Likewise, it you want to work out what percentage of profit there is when both the cost price and selling prices are known, divide the profit by the selling price and multiply by 100. For example, if an article costs 77p and sells for 88p, the profit is 11p, and the equation is 11/88 × 100 = 12.5 per cent.

Using POR you can never earn 100 per cent profit unless the article costs you nothing. Profit on cost is sometimes quoted by reps, and is a totally useless figure. It is always higher than POR, with no upward ceiling. For instance, if an item costs 50p and you sell it for £1.00 you are earning 100 per cent on cost, but only 50 per cent on return (50/100 × 100).

Working Out Retail Prices With VAT

If you want to earn a set percentage of profit on an item subject to VAT, are you clear in your mind as to whether you should do your calculations on the cost price exclusive of VAT or inclusive of VAT? Take the following example where you want to earn 20 per cent profit on an item costing £4.00 excluding VAT.

4/80 × 100 = Retail 5.00 plus VAT = £5.75
£4.00 + (VAT 15%) = 4.60/80 × 100 = £5.75.

In other words, it makes no difference at all as long as you remember the retail price follows the wholesale; i.e. if the wholesale price includes VAT, so will the retail, if it does not you will have to add it on to the retail. Use whichever system is easier at the time.

Forgetting to Add VAT to Retail Price

If you do forget to add the VAT element to a retail price it will upset your calculations and profit margins. For example, if you bought an item for 55p excluding VAT, and you want to earn 50 per cent POR, your calculation should be

$$\frac{55}{50} \times 100 = £1.10 + 15 \text{ per cent VAT} = £1.27.$$

If you forget to add the VAT your selling price will be £1.10 and your true percentage of profit 42.5 per cent because you will still have to pay VAT on the cost of 55p. If you think that is bad, just look what happens when you want to work on smaller margins!

40% would come down to 31%
35% would come down to 25%
30% would come down to 19½%
25% would come down to 13%
20% would come down to 8%
16% would come down to 3½%
12% you would actually lose about a penny per item
10% you would actually lose over 2p per item
and 5% would cost you almost 5½p every time you sold an item!

Ready Reckoner for Profit Percentages

If you wish to earn different percentages of profit on return from various goods, the following table, together with a calculator, will save a lot of time.

To use Multiply the cost price of the outer by the relevant figure, using either Table A (zero-rated goods, or standard-rated including VAT), or Table B (standard-rated goods which do not include VAT).

Examples (18 per cent POR required)

(1) Standard-rated, VAT exclusive price of £3.77 for 24 items, (3.77 × .0585) = 22p.
(2) Standard-rated, VAT inclusive price of £5.61 for 36 items, (5.61 × .0339) = 19p.
(3) Zero-rated, single item 64p (.64 × 1.2196) = 78p.

The table can also be used to find the percentage of profit if a retail price is selected at random. This is done by dividing the proposed retail price by the cost of the outer and then marrying this figure to the relevant percentage. For example, if an outer of 12 tins of standard-rated, VAT exclusive goods is purchased for £3.45, the profit margin at 39p each would be approximately 15 per cent (.39/3.45 = 1130. If they were sold for 48p, the POR would be approximately 31 per cent (.48/3.45) = 1391.

Short Cuts to Gross Profit Margins

Double cost price	= 50% on return
Add $\frac{1}{2}$ to cost price	= 33.3% on return
Add $\frac{1}{3}$ to cost price	= 25% on return
Add $\frac{1}{4}$ to cost price	= 20% on return
Add 1/5 to cost price	= 16.6% on return
Add 1/6 to cost price	= 14.3% on return
Add 1/10 to cost price	= 9% on return

Table A (Zero-rated and Standard-rated VAT inclusive prices)				Table B Standard-rated (VAT exclusive)			
% Single	12's	24's	36's	Singles	12's	24's	36's
1% 1.0101	.0842	.0421	.0281	1.1617	.0969	.0485	.0323
3% 1.0310	.0860	.0430	.0287	1.1856	.0988	.0494	.0330
5% 1.0527	.0878	.0439	.0293	1.2106	.1009	.0505	.0337
7% 1.0753	.0897	.0449	.0299	1.2366	.1031	.0516	.0344
9% 1.0990	.0916	.0458	.0306	1.2638	.1054	.0527	.0352
11% 1.1236	.0937	.0469	.0313	1.2922	.1077	.0539	.0359
13% 1.1495	.0958	.0479	.0320	1.3219	.1102	.0551	.0368
15% 1.1765	.0981	.0491	.0327	1.3530	.1128	.0564	.0376
16% 1.1905	.0993	.0497	.0331	1.3691	.1141	.0571	.0381
17% 1.2049	.1005	.0503	.0335	1.3856	.1155	.0578	.0385
18% 1.2196	.1017	.0509	.0339	1.4025	.1169	.0585	.0390
19% 1.2346	.1029	.0515	.0343	1.4198	.1184	.0592	.0395
20% 1.25	.1042	.0521	.0348	1.4376	.1198	.0599	.0400
21% 1.2659	.1055	.0528	.0352	1.4557	.1214	.0607	.0405
22% 1.2821	.1069	.0535	.0357	1.4744	.1229	.0615	.0410
23% 1.2988	.1083	.0542	.0361	1.4936	.1245	.0623	.0415
24% 1.3158	.1097	.0549	.0366	1.5132	.1261	.0631	.0421
25% 1.3334	.1112	.0556	.0371	1.5334	.1278	.0639	.0426
27% 1.3699	.1142	.0571	.0381	1.5754	.1313	.0657	.0438
29% 1.4085	.1174	.0587	.0392	1.6198	.1350	.0675	.0450
31% 1.4493	.1208	.0604	.0403	1.6667	.1389	.0695	.0463
33% 1.4926	.1244	.0622	.0415	1.7165	.1431	.0716	.0477
35% 1.5385	.1283	.0642	.0428	1.7693	.1475	.0738	.0492
40% 1.6667	.1389	.0695	.0463	1.9167	.1598	.0799	.0533
45% 1.8182	.1516	.0758	.0506	2.0910	.1743	.0872	.0581
50% 2.0000	.1667	.0834	.0556	2.3000	.1917	.0959	.0639
55% 2.2223	.1852	.0926	.0618	2.5556	.2130	.1065	.0710
60% 2.5000	.2084	.1042	.0695	2.8750	.2396	.1198	.0799
65% 2.8572	.2381	.1191	.0794	3.2858	.2739	.1370	.0913

If you look at the wholesale price per dozen, and charge the price shown by moving the decimal point one place to the left, you will earn 16.66 per cent on return. For example: £3.40 per dozen would be 34p each, but be careful of those lines carrying VAT in which case either add it to the wholesale price or the retail.

Price Flashed Products

Always ask and be aware of the profit margins on price flashed products, whether they be cat food, baked beans or biscuits. These margins are usually very low, sometimes practically non-existent. The choice is yours as to whether to stock them, feature them, or ignore them, but always remember what they are. One question you may like to ask, is 'Why is it that when a manufacturer wants to increase his sales and therefore his market share, and decides to print a lower price to help him do so, he expects the retailer to subsidise most of his promotion?' In the case where an average percentage is 10 per cent, and this is cut to 2 per cent, the retailer has to sell at least five times as many items to earn the same cash profit. Surely, if the manufacturer is promoting something, he should bear the brunt of the loss. It is obvious that they do not when they produce specially priced labels just for multiples at 2p or 3p less than for the independents.

Milk

Discounts on milk have traditionally been based on a set amount per gallon. This means that when there is a price increase your percentage of profit decreases, and when you ask your supplier for more money you are given the old 'hard luck' story that virtually all the increase is going to the farmers, the government, the EEC, etc., etc. To avoid this annual or biennial fiasco, try to arrange a fixed percentage discount so that when the price of milk increases, so will your cash discount.

Vacuum Packers

Using a vacuum packer to produce retail packs has to be judged on an entirely different basis to using the machine for prolonging the life of bulk foods which will later be sold loose across the counter. It is all too easy to set a price for these retail packs which at first sight appear to show a good margin of profit, but when analysed will not be anywhere near sufficient. Not only is there the cost of the bag to take into account, but also the labour costs and wear and tear on the machine. This last item can be very substantial. For instance, a new pump and motor on my bench model cost me over £600! If I packed 20 units a day, five days a week, for a whole year, I would have to add over 11p to each pack to get my money back. Labour costs need some time and motion study. Time how long it takes to finish a set number of packs, including labelling, and divide the wages rate per hour by this number. For example, if it takes 10 minutes to complete 20 packs, that equals 120 per hour. If you are paying your staff £2.50 per hour you would have to add at least 2p for labour:

Labour	2p
M/c Maintenance	11p
Cost of bag	5p
Total	18p

Therefore 18p needs to be added to each retail price. So, if you are packing approximately 4oz of ham which normally sells at £1.80 per pound, you should really weigh and price it at £2.52 per pound. (See also page 46.)

Stockroom

Keep your stockroom tidy and regularly go through the shelves to keep goods rotated and to make sure that you do not forget odd items.

Storage of Goods

Do not store or display foods next to strong smelling goods such as washing powders.

Stockroom Control

Filling the shelves in the shop will become much faster and thorough if you follow the ensuing method. You will also be able to see at a glance exactly what is out there at any time. Take a sheet of paper and rule it off, then draw a vertical line down the centre. Have several photocopies made to save the tedium of doing it over and over again. Giving each item in your stockroom a different line, write the name of the product and the number in stock. Put a circle round this number. When you come to fill the shop shelves take the sheet with you and make a note of the number required beside the circled one. Once these are removed from the stockroom the balance should be circled ready for the next time. As stock is put into the stockroom it should be automatically entered onto the sheet. This sheet should be kept on a large clipboard and hung up in a conspicuous place in the stockroom. Attach a pen to the clipboard by a piece of string. There will be the odd occasion when something has sold particularly fast and you need to run out to the stockroom for more, and forget, or do not have time to alter the sheet, but this will not really matter because the stockroom control sheet is not meant for these really fast selling lines, anyway.

Pricing Goods in Stockroom

To save time later, make sure that *all* goods are priced before they are put into the stockroom.

Stock

Stock Is Dead Money

Remember that money invested in stock is dead money until the stock is sold. If it does not sell, your cash is dwindling with inflation. You would be better off putting it into a building society.

Reduce Stock by £1,000

Most retailers could reduce their stock by at least £1,000 by being more careful with their ordering. If using the pricing gun strategy as suggested (see page 22) it will be possible to know exactly how fast each line is selling, and you will be able to say to yourself, "Do I really need to order 'x' this time, or have I got sufficient until the next order?" Remember, £1,000 saved on stock will allow you to introduce a new line, or will reduce your overdraft, or will earn more interest in the building society.

Ordering—Mark the Lines You Have

When ordering from an order book and faced with several different types of the same item, for example different flavours of Whiskas or Chum, it is much easier to put a dot beside each type you have in stock. You can then see what is missing immediately.

Buy Locally

Whenever possible, price permitting of course, buy your goods locally. Not only will this create more interest once the customer knows, it will also have the added benefit of being able to replenish stocks quickly and easily.

Order Sheet by Till
Keep a sheet of paper by the till to write down out of stock lines or odd items which need replenishing.

Cash and Carry

If you use a Cash and Carry spend a few minutes making a note of each of the shelving runs, numbering them and noting which goods are on each. Use this plan when making out your list of goods to buy and you will get done in half the time.

Two Suppliers

Better prices and quality can be obtained on goods such as eggs and fruit and vegetables if two suppliers are used. Each will try to be as competitive as possible to gain more custom.

Fresh Foods

Bear in mind that all fresh food, including greengrocery, deteriorates quickly and loses weight by evaporation the longer it is kept. So make sure there is a local demand for these kinds of goods before becoming committed to capital expenditure on fittings and equipment.

Budget Brand with Premium Brand

Try to rationalise your stock. It is not necessary to have six brands of baked beans and four of tinned potatoes; one own label or cheap brand alongside the market leader is quite sufficient, but make sure there is a choice of prices within a group of products.

Using Letters on Guns

How would you like to pick up any item in your shop and be able to tell immediately how long you have had it? This is very simple to do if you have a pricing gun of the type that has letters as well as numerals. Count each month as a separate letter—'A' = January, 'B' = February, 'C' = March, and so on. Change the letter on the first day of each month and you will soon see which lines are not selling, and as a bonus you will also be able to see which ones have not been rotated properly on the shelf!

Dispose of Largest Outers First

When you have a delivery, or return from a Cash and Carry, mark up and dispose of the largest boxes first, to provide more space and make the shop look as uncluttered as possible.

'Leakers'—Weighing

When you see a case that has a damp patch on it, or is sodden, it is very often difficult to tell whether this has been caused by one of the items inside the outer, or whether it has just been in contact with something else that has leaked. It does not matter whether it is a pack of milk, a tray of cans of beer, or a box of bleach, the solution is just the same. Weigh each individual item on the scale and you will soon find the culprit if it is there.

Displaying in Boxes

When displaying goods in boxes, you will find they have much more impact and look more attractive if the container is turned into a display box by cutting as shown below.

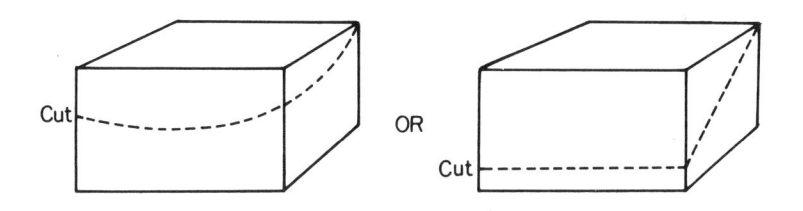

Open Boxes Upside Down When tipping out boxes of crisps, etc. into dump bins, open the boxes upside down so that when they are tipped out they face the right way.

Pre-packing—Price Per Pound

When pre-packing and pre-pricing goods for self selection, e.g. cheese in the chilled cabinets, bear in mind that price per pound is irrelevant as far as the customer is concerned. All he is interested in is the unit price. Therefore try to price up goods for, say, 50p or just under £1.

Just Over, Sir?

Are you a 'Just over, sir?' or a 'Little under, madam?' when weighing cheese, cold meats or confectionery? If you are the latter, the faster you turn into a 'Just over, sir?' the better. Work out how an extra ounce on average for each person adds up over the week. And, what is more, all at a high profit margin.

Weighing goods Make sure that whatever you are weighing does not touch or lean on anything other than the plate or scoop, or you will get a false reading which will probably not be in your favour.

Paper Bags

The cost of providing paper bags can be quite considerable when taken over a year. There is a great deal of difference between the price of the largest and the smallest. It makes sense, therefore, to keep a selection of bags of different sizes, and always use the smallest one possible for the goods you are selling. They will still cost you a lot of money, but at least you will know that you have not wasted any of it.

Merchandising

Whenever you have a few minutes to spare during the day, walk around the shop and take note of fixtures to clean and displays to be altered. Merchandise the shelves by making sure all items are the correct way up, not dusty, and brought to the front. If you have just three items stuck at the back of one of the bottom shelves the only type of person who will be able to see it will be someone only eighteen inches high. Bring them to the front where they can be seen. Likewise, stock on the top shelf should be brought to the front because not many people have eight foot long arms to reach the back of that shelf. Exercise commonsense; if the customer cannot see it, he will not ask for it. If he cannot reach it, he will not buy it.

Take Care of High Profit Lines

Although all the shelves should be merchandised, pay particular attention to those goods which are short dated, such as pies, sausages, bread and cakes, and constantly keep an eye on any high profit promotions you are running. This way you will keep wastage to a minimum and take more money on the lines you want to sell.

Check Dates Last Thing at Night

Get into the habit of checking the 'sell by' dates on bread, cakes and fresh food last thing at night when stocks are at a low level. It will not take very long, and will ensure that no one is able to complain 'I bought this this morning and it tasted peculiar, so I looked at the top, and it was yesterday's date on it.'

Goods in Short Supply

There are always problems when something is in short supply. Do not sell all your stock to someone you have never seen before—you will probably never see them again afterwards. Try to look after the regular customers, making sure at the same time that you do not actually get left with anything.

Customers Order Forms

Never take an order for a seasonal line without taking a deposit. One way of maximising sales and ensuring a deposit is to photocopy your own order forms. These need only be slips similar to those left by the milkman at Christmas, and should be headed by your hours of opening. After that list the most popular lines followed by a few blank spaces for additional ones. Complete the form by stating 'All orders must be accompanied by a minimum deposit of £1' and leave spaces for name, address and signature. Leave a pile of these by the till. If a customer asks you to put something aside, all you need say is 'Would you mind completing one of these forms? It makes it much easier for us to sort everything out later on.' You will be surprised at how many people will hand you a completed form together with a £1 coin. And any forms left over? Put a pile by the telephone and use them to write messages on.

STOCK RANGE AND MERCHANDISING

Bank Holiday Opening Hours

Generally speaking the customer does not bother to read lists of days and opening hours for a whole week, and when he does, he soon forgets. The best way of letting your customers know what hours you will be opening on a Bank Holiday, for instance, is to have a large notice on the front door simply stating 'BANK HOLIDAY—OPEN FROM 6.00a.m. to 12.30p.m. ONLY', or similar, and another notice of the same kind by the till.

Bank Holidays

Immediately after all Bank Holidays, especially the longer ones such as Christmas and Easter, the public will want to replenish their stock of necessities such as bread, milk, potatoes, and *lavatory paper*. Make sure to take full advantage by having plenty of stock ready for them.

Promotions and Pricing

Delayed Reactions

When doing a promotion or offering a new line, do not become too impatient if it does not reach your expectations immediately. Most sales are subject to a delayed reaction. It usually takes about a week for information to 'sink in'.

Displaying Carded Goods

Blank spaces on walls can be turned into display areas for carded goods if these are stuck on the wall either with doubled-sided sellotape or double-sided sticky pads, such as those used for fixing mirrors on to walls.

Sell High Profit Lines

Be aware of the lines that show the most cash profit and concentrate your efforts on selling these.

Increase Facings of Best Sellers

Increase the facings of the best selling lines. This should increase sales and make the task of stacking the shelves easier.

Sequential Sales or 'Chain Reactions'?

You can increase sales of some lines by encouraging sales of others. For example, if you persuade more people to eat bran breakfast cereals, you will sell more lavatory paper!

Do Not Compete on Price with the Multiples

Do not try to compete on price with the multiples—you will be playing into their hands. Your special offer prices on Heinz Baked Beans, Kelloggs Cornflakes, Robertsons Golden Shred, etc., will probably still be higher than the multiple's normal prices and will only show just how dear your own normal prices are. It is far better to make as much as you can on your own special offers on areas where the multiples are not strong, and where you can undercut them and still make a decent profit. Eggs, bacon and greengrocery are three examples.

3 for 39p, etc.

Whenever possible try to increase your sales by 'two for . . .', or 'three for . . .', but make sure you work your profit margin out on the discounted price. Do not do it the other way round. For example, if an item costs you 10p and you want to earn 23 per cent profit you could advertise it as 3 for 39p(23 per cent), or 14p each(28 per cent).

99p/£1, 59p/60p

Do not forget when pricing goods that 99p looks much less than £1, and 59p looks a lot less than 60p.

Dump Bins

The customer loves a bargain. If he sees a selection of items thrown haphazardly into a basket or dump bin with a large price ticket, he automatically assumes that it is a special offer. Take advantage of this to move slow selling lines or earn extra profit on others. For example, a notice saying 'Everything in this basket, only 99p each' will soon get the customer rummaging, and wondering if he could really do with a spare left-handed screwdriver. On the other hand, I have seen many customers sort out six small Kit Kats from a '10p' basket, which I had previously broken up from a pack of six, and which I still had on display at 52p!

Late Date Goods

If you are ever offered 'late date' goods at a special price by a supplier, do not cut your margins to the bone initially. Start by selling them at as high a price as you feel able to; then, when sales start to slow down, you will be able to clear the rest of the stock by reducing them even further. You could even go out at cost price or less, having made your profit initially.

If selling late date goods at a special price, keep them well away from the normal stock so that the customer will not be led into believing that your general lines are out of date. This can even be done in the food chiller with yoghurts and cream, etc., by making a special display and notice well away from the position at which these goods are normally kept.

Local Promotions

Work out some promotions of your own. Ask local suppliers if they have a surplus of a particular line and if they will reduce the price by 'x' amount so that you can do a promotion on it. Extra sales and goodwill can be achieved, and you will not be working on 2 per cent profit.

Charity Raffle

Try to earn some extra goodwill and free advertising by holding a raffle for a local charity, or for a piece of equipment needed by a local hospital, etc., and then make sure the press know all about it.

Only One Per Customer

Experiment with psychology. For instance, if you are overloaded with a certain line, make a nice display and put a notice on it saying 'Limited stock—only one per customer'. You will not sell any less than you did before, and you may sell a lot more.

Different Ways of Selling the Same Thing

Experiment with different ways of selling the same thing. As an example, I once made a special purchase of over one hundred outers of crisps in multi bags of six which were well in date but had an old design. Each pack of six contained two plain crisps, two cheese and onion, and two salt and vinegar. I made a large pile and priced them at 39p per pack. After a few days I could see it was going to take an eternity to clear all the stock, so I emptied a dozen bags into a trolley, placed it by the side of the pile and priced these at '10p each or 6 for 50p', retaining the '39p each' ticket on the bulk. Sales immediately took off, and I was absolutely amazed at the number of customers who selected two plain crisps, two cheese and onion, and two salt and vinegar from the trolley, even after seeing me break open the original bags!

Exotic Foods

Many extra sales can be made by stocking some of the more exotic sounding foods, but there are three golden rules to look out for here:

(1) Make sure the quantity you have to buy can be sold before the 'sell by' date.
(2) Make a special display and talk about the goods to your customers.
(3) Try to order foods which, if all else fails, you can eat yourself.

Cold Drinks Cabinets

If you have the space, a cold drinks chiller will certainly increase your canned drink sales during sunny weather. If you do not, try to make room in a dairy cabinet or serveover. If you also have a cold room it is a good idea to keep a stock of drinks there ready chilled for that extra hot spell.

Soft Drinks 'Reserve'

Towards the end of May is a good time to build up a reserve stock of canned and fizzy drinks. These are good money earners, and as it is impossible to judge what the British summer is going to be like, it is as well to be prepared because you can bet your life that if a two week heatwave came along wholesalers and manufacturers would not be able to supply.

Seasonal Lines

Keep an eye on seasonal lines at holiday times and ensure they are prominently displayed, especially for the last few days running up to the holiday. If you think you have over ordered, reduce the prices. If goods are left after the holiday, you will have to reduce them by a lot more to dispose of them!

Mother's Day/Father's Day, etc.

Take full advantage of Mother's Day, Father's Day, Valentine's Day, etc., by making a special display of anything in stock which might suit. Write out a notice 'IDEAS FOR FATHER'S DAY' or something similar, and site it prominently in the shop. This is an ideal method for disposing of some of the 'slow movers'.

Christmas Stock

At Christmas time try to create more impact by displaying all your Christmas lines together.

Hampers

Have you ever thought of doing your own Christmas Hampers? The advantages are enormous and far outweigh the old Christmas Clubs because you receive full price for everything you include. Lists will have to be printed, of course, but if you have access to a photocopier this will be a very minor expense. Get some ideas by looking at the existing hamper companies and milkman's brochures.

Clear Out After Christmas

Once Christmas is over you will have a good opportunity to sort out your general stock. Collect together any lines which are slow selling and which you have decided not to repeat, together with any Christmas lines left over, and raffle them or reduce to clear.

STOCK RANGE AND MERCHANDISING

Remove Tatty Goods

Keep an eye on the shelves for dented or tatty goods and remove them immediately. If you cannot get credit from your supplier, reduce them sufficiently to clear.

Reduce and Dispose of Lines that Do Not Sell

If you are using the dating method on pricing tickets (see page 22) you will soon see which lines are not selling. Check through regularly and make a mental note not to reorder any item the sales of which are perhaps less than one per month. If you see a line that is standing completely still it may be better to reduce it to clear thus making your money available for something else.

Wastage Not only are laughter and misery infectious, but so is your outlook towards wastage. If you adopt a 'couldn't-care-less', 'throw it away' attitude, so will your staff, and they will probably throw away a lot more than you. It is only a short step from there to set them thinking that "this seems too good to throw away, I will take it home instead", then you will really see your profits go down. It is much better to let staff think you are a miserly old so-and-so trying to get the last dregs of profit from all the odd ends, dusty or shop soiled remnants.

Facings on Shelves

Are you losing sales and making hard work for yourself filling shelves and fixtures? Take a good look around your shop and reduce all slow moving lines to one facing and increase the space devoted to the best sellers. You will gain both from higher sales and less work stocking the shelves.

Psychology Again

Take the four aces from a pack of playing cards and lay them face down in front of someone you know, and ask him to pick out the Ace of Diamonds. In most cases he will choose the inside right position, and if you have made sure the Ace of Diamonds is there, you will be looked at with astonishment. You may ask, 'What has this got to do with merchandising?', the answer is very simple. If you want the customer to choose one particular item, perhaps because it was the last of the old stock, place it in the 'inside right' position, as shown below.

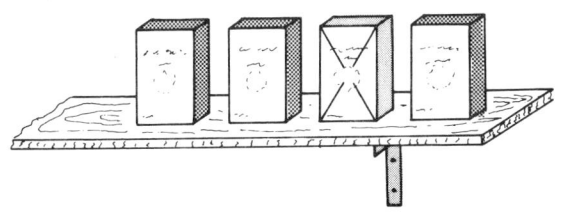

Changing Positions of Stock

If a particular line is not selling, try changing its position in the shop. It is amazing how often this does the trick.

Add New Lines

You may find that after rationalisation of this sort you have sufficient space in the shop to introduce some completely new type of goods.

New Line

When offered a brand new product do not order a large amount initially, especially if it has a 'sell by' date, unless of course it is at a giveaway price and if the worst comes to the worst you can at least get your money back. Remember, new products are continually being produced. Very few of them last after the initial television advertising comes to an end. Generally speaking it's the old favourites that continue to sell.

When considering taking on a new line or range that requires a heavy investment, do not be influenced by the vociferous few, but ask as many of your customers as possible for their opinions, or even have a questionnaire photocopied and distributed. Decide whether it is a viable proposition or not when all the information is obtained.

Other Shops

If you go out for the day and see something of interest in another shop, do not be afraid to introduce yourself to the shopkeeper and ask for the name and address of the supplier.

Opposition

It is always a good idea to keep an eye on the opposition, not necessarily to be influenced by them, but just to know what is going on elsewhere.

Larger Sizes

Try stocking some of the largest sizes of the most popular lines—pet food, washing powders, etc. The customer is a peculiar creature. If he comes into your shop to buy a giant size, and you have not got one, he will not buy two small items even if they work out to the same price as a large one. He will either buy one, or none at all.

Smaller sizes Take note of the sizes of goods that you are selling. You might find that you can increase sales by catering for certain sections of the community e.g. some smaller sizes for old age pensioners living alone.

Do not think that because a large size is only a penny or two more the customer will buy that instead. To some people economics just do not count. If they have come out to buy a small size, then that is what they want, regardless. I remember an occasion when I made a special purchase of large tins of soup and priced them much cheaper than the small ones. Several people still refused to buy them, and when I suggested that at that price they could afford to eat what they like, throw the rest away, and still save money, they looked at me as if I was mad.

Health and Beauty and Home Medicines

If you do not have a chemist near you, do not neglect the 'Health and Beauty and Home Medicine' market. This is a very substantial sector and has the dual benefit of relatively high unit values and good profit margins. Retail price maintenance on home medicines means that you can sell them for the same price as the superstores.

Hiring

If there is no local opposition consider hiring out equipment such as carpet cleaners, ladders, DIY equipment, punch bowls and cups, cake stands and knives, etc.

Agencies

Keep an eye open for opportunities of becoming an agent for services such as dry cleaning, shoe repairs, clock repairs, photographic processing, and even perhaps, insurance.

Seeds, Compost, Plants, etc

Another area to explore, if there is no local competition, is that of seeds and gardening requisites. Some suppliers can provide a display rack for seeds, and offer sale or return terms at the end of the season. You need not stop at seeds; grow bags, fertilisers, potting composts etc. can be displayed outside the shop. You could introduce bedding plants, heathers, conifers, and even small shrubs if you have the space.

School Uniforms

If there is a school nearby that has a school uniform, find out where the nearest suppliers are and see if there is an opening for you in this field. A visit to the headmaster would help, as would an advertisement in any school programmes for events during the year. Needless to say, these are all good profit lines.

Calor Gas

Calor Gas is another area to be explored if there are no stockists nearby. Whether it is worthwhile or not depends on your area, but quite a lucrative trade can be built up in the right position and apart from the cylinders there is also the Camping Gaz range of fuel and accessories.

Secondhand Books

Selling secondhand paperback books can be profitable. You can either do it on a library basis, i.e. the customer buys a book and gets a part refund on it when another is purchased, or it can be done on a straight 'two for one' exchange basis.

Lottery Tickets

If you sell lottery tickets be careful how many are on display at one time if they are in a position where they can be reached by the customer. It is very easy to take 10 or 20 at a time, and at 20p or 25p each, this can work out very expensive. It is wiser to have just two or three on display, and to replenish the holder from bulk stock which is kept out of sight.

Bedsitters

If there are a lot of bedsitters near to the shop, if may pay to increase your range of convenience foods and ready meals, or even devote part of the shop solely to this area.

'End Pieces'

If you have a cold food counter in your shop, do you have problems disposing of the end pieces? An excellent solution to this is to make up a few filled rolls and sandwiches, wrap them in cling film, price them, and place on the counter or in a dairy cabinet. Apart from the obvious sales to workmen, schoolchildren, etc., you will be surprised at how many of your regular customers and even old age pensioners will buy them. And any that do not sell—have them for your own lunch!

Sandwich Deliveries

If your shop is situated near to schools, factories or offices it may pay dividends to enquire whether you could deliver sandwiches direct to their place of business. Once you have a base you could then spread your wings. With profit margins of over 50 per cent you could really take off.

CHAPTER 3

Reps and Delivery Men

'Opportunity makes the thief.'

Sales Representatives

Paying

If a rep you have never seen before suddenly appears in your shop, on no account pay him any cash, unless he actually brings in goods and gives you a receipt. *Always* get a receipt if you pay a rep.

Payment in Advance

Never, ever, pay for goods or services in advance. If a company is trading in this manner, it has obvious cash flow problems and could go bankrupt at any time, or it could be just a big con.

Discounts

If you are not satisfied with the rate of discount offered, do not be afraid to ask for more. He can only say 'No'.

Ordering

Never feel under any obligation or allow yourself to be pressurised by a rep. If you are undecided tell them you want time to think about it and that you will contact them.

Off-the-Cuff Claims by Salesmen

Do not believe off-the-cuff claims by salesmen. Many of them will say anything to get a sale, and a good proportion will not know anything about the equipment anyway.

Confirm Everything in Writing

Never assume anything. Get everything in writing so that all parties understand clearly. The easiest way to do this is to write a letter of confirmation to the company listing everything you expect to be done or to be provided with. Keep a photocopy of this letter in a safe place in case you need it at a later date.

Sale or Return

If you are offered 'sale or return', find out exactly what is meant. Does it mean that he will put stock into your shop free of charge and you only pay for what has been sold, or does it mean that you have to buy the initial stock and he will uplift any lines that do not sell? If so, will new lines be replaced there and then, or will a credit note be given? What happens if the whole display does not sell? If in the slightest doubt ask for everything to be put in writing.

Deliveries

If you have deliveries in crates or trays, such as milk, bread, cakes, pies, bottles of beer, etc., do not just count the containers, but lift each off and look underneath, because if there is going to be shortage, that is where it will be. Always check deliveries before signing or paying for them.

Collections

Never allow any goods or equipment that belongs to you, or that you have signed for, to be removed from the shop by a rep or driver without receiving a collection note from them.

Orders

Do not allow a delivery man to make out his own order and place it on the shelves without checking it as it comes into the shop. Then make sure he walks out empty-handed!

Trusting Your Friendly Roundsman

Do not trust anyone, especially roundsmen, and especially extra friendly roundsmen. Being friendly does not make them dishonest, but it can make you complacent and accept everything as correct without checking. This is fine until the roundsman finds himself short of a few pennies, and then ... This can very quickly become habit forming and can cost you hundreds of pounds over the course of a year.

Delivery Men's Tricks

One trick a delivery man may carry out is to come into the shop and take stock of his own lines as if making an order, and whilst doing this he makes a special note of one or two items already on the shelf, and orders them again. He makes up the delivery in the van, less these items, and balances the books when he comes into the shop by adding your stock to his delivery when you are not looking, and before you check it off. If you suspect this may be happening to you, the easiest way of finding out is either to count the number of items on the shelf before he comes in to make up the order, or if there are not too many, to put a special mark on each. This type of fraud usually only happens with pre-priced goods where you do not have to use your own pricing labels.

Proof of Orders

If a company delivers goods and asks for payment for something you do not want and cannot remember ordering, or sends an invoice for some sort of service you did not require, such as an entry into a trades directory, do not just pay up, ask to see written proof of your order.

Merchandising

It never hurts to ask van drivers or reps for suggestions as to merchandising their products on your shelves. You don't have to take their advice, but it is always interesting to note how other stores, both large and small, display their stock.

Messages on Nails/Hooks

How many times do you say to yourself, after a rep has left your shop, 'I forgot to tell him about so-and-so!' If you have a super memory this will not apply to you, but if you have not, there is a simple answer. Find a clear piece of wall, preferably near to the telephone, and bang in half a dozen or so nails at six or seven inch intervals. Whenever you think to yourself 'I must tell the . . . rep about this' scribble it onto a piece of paper and stick it on an appropriate nail. A quick glance at this in passing will keep you on the ball. Use it for customer orders and saves.

CHAPTER 4

Customer Relations

'Civility costs nothing.'

Selling to the Customer

The main object of standing in a shop all day is to take money. Everything you do should be towards that aim. If you just want to chat all day long, you may as well sit on a park bench and talk to passers-by.

Customer's Appearance

Do not take too much notice of a customer's appearance. At the end of the day his money is worth just as much as anyone else's. It could even be said that the less money he spends on clothing and hair-do's, the more he will have to spend in your shop!

Obnoxious Customers

We are all in business to take money. We are also self-employed because we obtain a certain job satisfaction from running a shop. Unfortunately, this job satisfaction is sometimes marred by the odd obnoxious customer. We should remember again however, that when the till is totalled at the end of the day, his money is no different to anyone else's. Why not resolve, for a few days at least, to be extra friendly to those customers you most detest? You may be in for a pleasant surprise!

Smile

Smile and greet each customer as they come into your shop. You may not be able to stand the sight of them, *but*, they have chosen to come into your shop and they have brought their money with them.

CUSTOMER RELATIONS

New Feature Each Week

Try to keep the inside of the shop looking different, and the customers interested, by featuring something new each week.

Happy Shop—Price Comparisons

Probably the biggest objection the customer has to shopping in your shop, is price. By having a happy shop and being pleasant to the customer you will help to overcome this and to distract the customer from making price comparisons.

Do Not Let the Customer Wait

Never make a customer wait whilst you finish doing some paperwork, or cleaning, and never carry on doing it whilst serving.

Uniform

A uniform is important in a shop. Customers should be able to distinguish easily and quickly who is a member of staff, and who is not.

Place Article in Customer's Hands

Sales can be effected much easier if the article in question is placed into the customer's hands. If you can get him to hold it, you are halfway to selling it.

It's Still . . . .

You may find it helps a sale if, when a customer asks the price of something, you reply 'It's *still* . . .'. This may convey to the customer that it is an old price and he may be getting a bargain, or averting an impending increase.

Free Delivery

Quite often a free delivery service will encourage your customer to spend more than he originally intended. You should set a lower limit though, or you might be asked to deliver the odd packet of sugar that he forgot to buy at Tesco!

Enthusiasm

To sell a product to the customer you need to show enthusiasm. Enthusiasm only comes from knowledge, so the more knowledge you have of a group of products, whether they be wines, cheeses, DIY products or knitting wools, the more you will sell.

Extra Sales

Try to sell something extra to every customer who comes into your shop. If one in ten spend an extra £1, you will take £10 extra per 100 customers per day. That means if you have 300 customers per day, six days a week, you will take an extra £180 weekly, or £9,360 per year, and at a good margin of profit.

'Have you seen our special offer on . . ., Mrs X?' 'Have you tried/tasted that new product . . . advertised on the television?', etc., etc. These are ways of getting extra sales. Think of it as doing the customer a favour—after all, if you did not tell him, he would probably never know.

Extra Sales from High Profit Lines

The customer will not like to be followed around the shop by you trying to sell a hundred and one lines, so do not bother with special offers and low profit lines—there is not much gain in that. Concentrate instead on trying to sell high profit lines only.

Suggestions

Listen to what a customer has to say and see if it suggests something he ought to buy. For instance, if a mother starts talking about her Jimmy being off school with a cough, you could suggest she tries some of your Brand X Cough Syrup with added Vitamin C; you have been told it is very good, and kids love it.

Alternatives

Always suggest an alternative if you have not got what the customer is looking for. For example, if you have sold out of cheese sauce, suggest he buys a packet of white sauce and grates some cheese into it. Tell him he will probably prefer it that way anyway!

Linked Sales

Try making 'linked' sales. For instance, if a customer buys a tin of furniture polish, ask if he needs some new dusters; if he buys a sponge pudding he may need custard or cream; small cake mixes need papercups; chickens need stuffing and bread sauce; paint and brushes need white spirit, etc.

Holidays

Pay attention to the seasons and holidays. For instance, a few days before Pancake Day you might make a large display of batter mix, eggs and lemons by the checkout and ask each customer, 'Have you bought your batter mix, eggs and lemons for Pancake Day yet? We have a special offer of . . . at the moment. How many would you like?' (See also 'Seasonal Lines' page 28.)

Closing the Sale

The most important part of your job is 'closing' the sale. Once the customer has shown agreement to buy, get the transaction over as quickly as possible. If you stand for another five minutes talking about it, he may change his mind.

Suggestions Box

Are you for ever thinking of ways to improve your business and perhaps continually looking for new lines to stock? One way of finding out what your customers think of the shop and what they would like to see on your shelves is to have a suggestion box on your counter. Mind you, you may need a thick skin when you come to read what they have written!

Customers' Special Requests

How many times have you been asked to stock a special item for a customer, then never see him again or be told that the product is too dear? One answer is to tell the customer that he will have to buy it in bulk and pay for half the order in advance. This way, if only half the order is purchased the remaining half will not cost too much considering the profit you have already taken. If the customer refuses to do this, you will in all probability have saved yourself from stocking another 'dead' line.

Customer Complaints

'Yes, But . . .'

The polite way of dealing with a customer's objections has always been 'Yes, but . . .'. This allows you to agree with him up to a point, but then to put forward your own point of view without appearing rude. Keep it in mind if the occasion arises with a customer you want to keep. If you are not bothered (it is a terrible thing to say, but we are all human) it does not matter what you reply.

Complaints—Make Sure Bought From You Originally

If a customer complains about goods, make sure he bought them from your shop before you do anything. Do not just take his word for it, but compare the pack to those on your shelves. It is surprising how many of these 'complaints' are not really your fault, but are only brought in because the customer cannot be bothered to go back to where he bought them from.

Customer Problems

Remember that although customers will tell you their problems and expect you to listen, most of them could not care less about your problems.

The Customer and Money

Security

The simple answer is 'do not give credit to anyone.' However, the simplest answers are not always the easiest to carry out. In my experience those asking for credit fall into two main categories: there are those who can manage their affairs most of the time but occasionally find themselves short; and there are those who continually live beyond their means, borrowing from everyone to finance their drinks/drugs/gambling problems. These are a hopeless group longterm. How do you find out which group a person belongs to? If you are new to an area, in most cases this is not possible. The safest method, if tempted to give credit, is to ask for something of value as security. No security, no credit. After all, if the customer will not trust you with his valuables, why should you trust him with your money?

Cheque with a Banker's Card

One possible solution for those who ask for credit and have a bank account with a banker's card, is for them to write a cheque to you for an agreed amount, you keep a running total of their purchases until this figure is reached, and then you bank it.

Unsigned Cheques

Beware of companies or individuals who tend to send cheques without a signature. Whilst this omission is occasionally accidental, everyone knows that this is a well-used ploy to gain a few extra days without having to pay. In other words, their bank balance is not too good.

Collecting Debts

If you do find yourself with a bad debt, you have three options:

(a) You can forget about it.
(b) You can try to collect it yourself.
(c) You can give the debt to a debt collecting agency.

Probably the cheapest and quickest way is to try to collect the debt yourself. Do not bother writing letters or telephoning, the only way to get results is to go round and knock loudly on the door. If you are *fobbed off* with an excuse, call back a few days later. And keep calling back. If you decide on a debt collecting agency find out if they are used to your type of business, what their charges are, and how often they will settle with you.

'I'll Bring the Odd Money Back.'

If a customer finds he is 20p or 30p short of what he needs to buy his goods and says he will bring the odd money back straightaway, do you agree and then forget all about it when he does not return? The easiest way out of this situation is to say that you do not want to *disrupt the till roll*, and it would be simpler if he left behind an item for that amount and then collected it when he brought the odd money back. This would keep your till straight. The customer has to agree or admit that he did not intend to bring the money back anyway. Children are probably the main culprits of this attempt to reduce your profits. Remember, you are not just letting them off 30p worth of takings, you are actually giving them 30p out of your wages.

Asking Customers to Do Things

Finally, think twice before accepting a customer's offer to mend your car/washing machine, to install double glazing, renew your electric wiring, etc., etc. In my experience these people fall mainly into two categories: there are those who are out of work and do not know what they are doing; and there are those who do it for a living, but will have to squeeze you in at odd times or weekends. Neither person will probably be able to do a good job in the time you want it done, and if you tell them what you think of them you will probably end up by losing a customer.

CHAPTER 5

Popular Trades

'Keep your shop and your shop will keep you.'

Grocers

'Lend your money and lose your friend.'

Guidelines

The following are some useful guidelines to enable you to work out how efficient your store is:

(1) Most grocery shops work on between 13 per cent and 18 per cent gross profit.
(2) Overheads should take care of 9 to 10 per cent of this figure, although there may be exceptions due to very high or low rental figures.
(3) Total wage bills should account for approximately 40 per cent of the gross profit. This should include a figure for your own wages at the rate for managers laid down by the Wages Council.
(4) After all expenses you should be left with approximately five per cent net profit.
(5) You should be taking at least £4 per square foot. The smaller the shop, the easier this figure is to take.
(6) Each checkout is capable of taking £10,000 per week. To avoid queues, instead of putting in another checkout think about having someone calling out prices and packing as well as the till operator. Customers like the idea because they believe you are helping them.
(7) Norms for multiples: In 1986 the norm for multiples was as follows:

Sales per square foot = £9.00 Sales per employee = £1,600 per week.
Wage costs = 6.4 per cent of turnover.

Potential Trade

To determine the potential grocery trade in a residential area, count the number of houses in the catchment area (say, a half mile radius) and multiply by £20 per house. This will give a rough approximation of the total available. Determine what percentage of that figure you are likely to get, taking into consideration proximity and size of other shops. As an example, if there are 1,253 houses in your catchment area and you hope to get 20 per cent of the trade, the formula would be: 1,253 × 20 × 20% = £5,012 per week.

Future Alternatives

The grocery business is one of the easiest to get into. Because of this, there is increasing competition both from small private shops and large superstores. If the only way you can survive is by reducing your profit margins and opening longer hours, you should think seriously of looking for another shop. The more hours you open, the less money you take per hour. Not all grocery shops face the same bleak future. Apart from them there are confectioner, tobacconist and newsagents (CTN's) and off licences. These are not subject to the same level of price cutting. There are also service industries such as dry cleaning, video rental, and instant print, perhaps even petrol stations which have some opportunity of adding a general type shop.

Delicatessens and Delicatessen Counters

'Waste not, want not.'

Dairy Facts

The average milk consumption per day in this country is approximately half a pint with skimmed and semi-skimmed sales becoming more and more popular, although still far below full cream varieties. There are strict hygiene regulations concerning the production and distribution of milk. All fresh milk put out for sale to the public must come from tuberculin-tested cows. An explanation of the different types of milk is as follows:

Pasteurised milk accounts for the bulk of milk sales. During this process the milk is heated to approximately 72° C(162° F) for 15 seconds killing off most bacteria.

Homogonised milk differs from pasteurised in that the fat globules are distributed evenly throughout the milk and do not rise to the top as cream.

Sterilised milk is prepared from homogonised milk which is bottled and then heated to approximately 120° C(248° F) for between 20 and 60 minutes. It has a slightly different taste and lasts longer.

UHT (Ultra High Temperature) milk is heated to approximately 130° C(266° F) for one or two seconds, and then packed into special containers which protect the milk from both light and oxygen. It will keep unopened for several months without refrigeration, but once it has been opened it has the same life as fresh milk.

Skimmed milk has almost all of its fat removed.

Semi-skimmed milk must contain between 1.5 per cent and 1.8 per cent fat.

The average bottle of milk contains 3.9 per cent milk fat. Milk from Jersey and Guernsey cows contains more, approximately 4.5 per cent. It also contains more vitamins and minerals.

Cream regulations are as follows:

Half Cream must contain at least 12 per cent milk fat.
Single Cream must contain at least 18 per cent milk fat.
Whipping Cream must contain at least 35 per cent milk fat.
Double Cream must contain at least 48 per cent milk fat.
Clotted Cream must contain at least 55 per cent milk fat.

Butter must not contain less than 78–80 per cent milk fat and not more than 16 per cent water.

Margarine can be made from a mixture of any edible oils and fats which have been homogonised with brine. All margarines offered for retail sale must by law have certain amounts of Vitamins A and D added.

Cheese

Temperature

The correct temperature for keeping cheese is 3° – 6° C or 36° – 42° F. Check your temperatures with a thermometer.

Life of Cheese

Hard cheeses such as Cheddar and Parmesan have a much longer life than moist cheeses such as Wensleydale, Cheshire, and Lancashire.

Displaying

(1) When arranging a cheese display try to have a variety of colour and shape, and garnish with accompaniments such as celery, grapes, wine, tomatoes, etc.
(2) Display cheese by country of origin rather than type, with the largest cheeses at the back and either end.
(3) As Cheddar is likely to be the biggest seller, arrange this in bulk at the far end of the cabinet so that the customer's eyes are drawn over the whole display.
(4) Mark cheeses which are low in calories accordingly and point this out to anyone who is talking about slimming.
(5) Try to have one or two of the slower selling cheeses on special offer every week to encourage customers to try them.
(6) Keep the customers' interest by adding new cheeses each month. New cheeses will also increase sales of those varieties placed next to them, so move the slowest sellers into these positions.
(7) A detailed description of each cheese will be appreciated by the customer and will increase sales.
(8) Encourage customers to try new cheeses by offering 'tasters'.
(9) Price unusual and expensive cheeses per quarter.

Cutting Cheese

It is not too difficult to cut half a pound or a pound of cheddar cheese, but what if you are asked for 1 ¾ lb or a £1 worth, or a piece of pie for 85p? This is just as simple if you weigh or price the entire piece and then judge accordingly. For instance, if the lump of cheese weighs 3lbs, then half of it will be 1 ½ lb. So if you cut slightly larger, you will not be too far wrong. It is the same when dealing with cash. If the whole piece costs £3.70, then half of it would be £1.85, a quarter 92p. A fraction larger would be about £1.

Look At What You Have Left When cutting a piece of cheese, etc., pay just as much attention to what will be left as to what you are about to sell, because if you leave a very small or odd shaped piece it may be difficult to sell it. If this is the case, tell the customer and cut the required amount from a more suitable piece.

Cutting Edam Score the rind of an Edam with a knife before cutting with a cheese wire. This will save your arm muscles as well as your pocket in replacing broken cheese wires.

Cover cut surfaces with cling film Cover all cut faces of cheese with cling film to stop them drying out. As most cheeses contain up to 50 per cent water, a lot of drying out can take place.

Cheeseboards Get into the habit of cleaning the cheeseboard and wire immediately after cutting blue cheeses or Edam. The first may transfer a smell to delicate flavoured cheeses that are cut immediately after, and the second will leave a thin coating of red rind on the wire which will stick to the face of the next cheese which is cut.

Meat

Home Cooked Ham

The most important and 'best earner' in a delicatessen cabinet is home cooked ham. These are very easy to do and not only provide something personal to your shop, but have high volume sales, a high unit price, and, most importantly, high profit margins. Full instructions for cooking ham will be found in the *bacon* section (see page 52).

Opening Tins of Meat

Opening large tins of meat for cutting (corned beef, luncheon meat, etc.) can be a particularly hazardous operation, as well as extracting the meat from the can. These problems will disappear if the tin is held under hot running water for a few seconds after opening. Do not leave it too long though, or you will have terrible trouble catching it as it slips out!

Cooked and Uncooked—Separate Utensils

Do not forget the hygiene rules that apply to 'open' food. Not only do cooked and uncooked meats have to be displayed separately, but they also have to be stored in such a manner so that there will be no contact between them. You will also need separate tongs, knives, and slicers.

Food Labelling Regulations

Under the Food Labelling Regulations Act 1986 retailers are obliged to display the name of the product, additives not excused by the regulations and the moisture content of meat products.

Write 'Sell By' Dates on Back of Tickets

When placing cooked meats, quiches, etc. in the serve-over, write the 'sell by' date on the back of the price ticket so that you know exactly where you stand according to the manufacturer.

Vacuum Packing

A vacuum packer is a most useful adjunct to the traditional serve-over counter. The only problems with them are the initial cost, the cost of repairs, and the fact that if they go wrong you cannot pack any more until the machine is repaired. (See also page 19.) You will also need labels displaying the name of the product, the weight, the price per pound, the price to be charged, and a 'sell by' date.

The Advantages

(1) It provides another point of sale so that customers do not have to queue up or wait. If they are in a hurry they can select a pack and be on the way to the checkout in less time than it takes you to put a lump of ham on the slicing machine.
(2) Anyone who can slice and weigh is able to use the machine. It is simply a matter of popping the product into a special packing bag, placing it in the machine, and pressing a button, turning a dial, or closing the lid.
(3) The bags are expensive, but even so you will still make a higher margin of profit selling at a lower price than the usual proprietory brands.
(4) Because vacuum packing keeps the product in good condition for weeks and weeks, you are able to offer a much larger range without the fear of wastage.
(5) The packing itself can be done at any slack time in the shop.
(6) Food lines which are ideal for vacuum packing are bacon, cheese, ham, cooked meats including paté, liver sausage, pork pie with egg, etc., etc. Other things which are not so obvious can also be vacuum packed, such as a few cream crackers, a pot of butter, cheese triangle, and a plastic knife on a tray or paper plate to make a picnic or office lunch. Frozen vegetables can also be bought in bulk and packed in smaller weights.
(7) Fresh meat can also be vacuum packed—pork, chicken, and lamb look very good, but red meat turns a very dark colour. However, once it has been taken out of the vacuum bag and oxygen gets to the blood it soon recovers and becomes red again.
(8) Slices of meats such as corned beef and tongue should be prevented from sticking together by separating each slice with a small piece of Finoplas.
(9) If you pack on the premises there is no need to list the ingredients of each product on the label so long as you have a list of ingredients nearby.
(10) Some retailers have found vacuum packing so successful they have done away with a serve-over altogether and installed another dairy cabinet instead.

Cutting

Sharp Knives

A sharp knife is much less dangerous than a blunt one because much less effort is needed to use it.

Using a Knife

Do not push a knife through the food you are cutting, rather regard it as a saw and use the whole length of the blade in a backward and forward motion allowing the edge to do the work.

Cutting Downwards

When slicing downwards, keep your fingertips on the end of your fingers by holding the food as shown below. The back of the knife should rest against the flat of your knuckles.

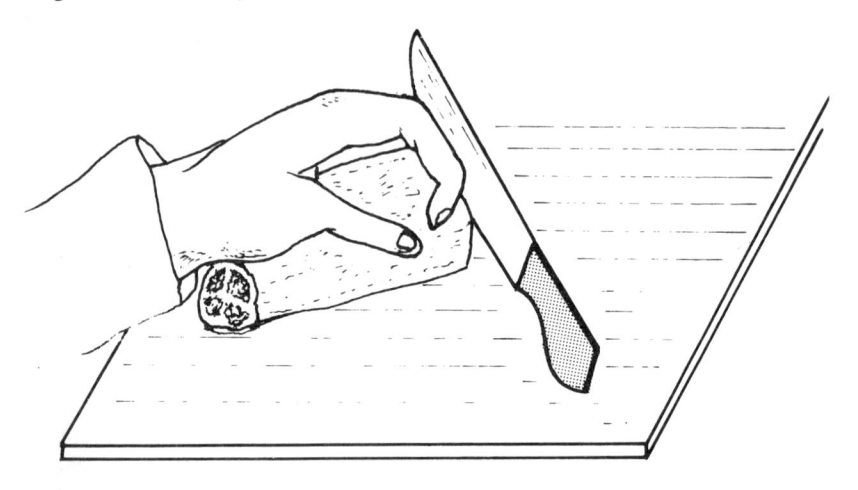

Slicing by Hand

When slicing by hand always start the cut at the outside edge and finish at a slightly downward angle. This ensures you get larger slices from the food and avoids bits. It is also far safer because there is less danger of cutting yourself.

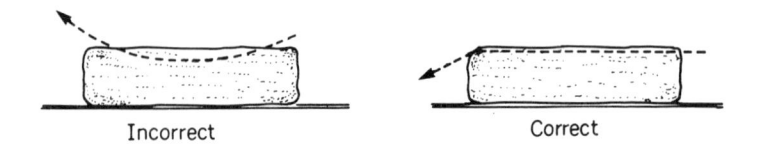

Incorrect

Correct

POPULAR TRADES

Slicing Cooked Meats

If the lump of meat you are cutting on your slicer tends to end up at an angle, you should turn it the other way round when next placing it on the slicer. This will keep it level and neat.

Cleaning and Hygiene

Cleaning Plastic Ticket Marks, etc.

If you have difficulty in removing marks from plastic pricing tickets, trays, etc., try using an abrasive cleaning powder and fine steel wool.

Refrigerated Counters

Most refrigerated counters have a drainage hole and a tube directed into a container for catching drips of water. Food particles are often carried into this container and can stay there for some considerable time, so it is not unusual for a foul odour to come from this area, especially when the water is thrown away. The answer is, of course, to empty it far more frequently, but in case you still forget (out of sight, out of mind), pour some neat strong bleach into the container and leave it there. This should do the trick.

Bleach

In sinks Sinks used for food preparation, as opposed to sinks for washing hands, can occasionally develop a smell from the plug hole. If this happens, pour neat bleach down the hole when you close the shop and leave it all night.

Bleaching cloths There is no need to throw away dishcloths once they become a little discoloured. Instead, take a plastic bucket and pour some neat strong bleach into the bottom. Drop the cloths in and add sufficient hot water to just cover the cloths. A long handled plastic sink brush is ideal for stirring the cloths around and serves the dual purpose of cleaning the bristles at the same time. This is also an ideal time to put in any nail brushes that need cleaning. Leave everything to soak for a suitable length of time, and *do not put unprotected hands into the bucket to wring out the cloths*! Rinse well before using again.

Taking Care of Yourself

Remember, slicing machines, whether electric or hand operated, can be extremely dangerous. If someone speaks to you or tries to catch your attention whilst you are cleaning the blade, ignore them. It is better to lose a sale than lose a finger! He will understand later when you explain to him.

Meat slicers Again, ignore anyone who speaks to you when you are cleaning a meat slicer, particularly the blade. If you allow yourself to be distracted for one second from what you are doing it could be lethal. Meat slicers are perfectly safe when handled properly. If you take chances, they can be very, very dangerous.

Cleanness of Counters

Cleanness is important throughout the delicatessen counter. Remember that you are selling fresh unwrapped food. Take a look from the customer's side. Would you want to buy unwrapped cooked meats and cheeses from your counter?

Mañana

Do not put off until tomorrow what you should do today, especially with regard to food. If you see something starting to look a little seedy, do something with it immediately—it will look far worse tomorrow, and worse still the day after, and you will end up by throwing it away. Take the bull by the horns, either trim it or put a special price on it, but get rid of it.

Fit for Human Consumption?

If you are ever faced with the question 'Is this item of food alright to sell, or is it past it?', ask yourself the ultimate question, 'Would I eat it?'. Your reply to this question will tell you the answer.

Licking Fingers

Do not lick your fingers before picking up bags, sheets of paper, etc., and never ever before picking up food. Do not lick them afterwards either even if part of the fresh cream cake lands on your finger!

Christmas Decorations

If you decorate the shop at Christmas time make sure none of the decorations can drop or be knocked off on to fresh open food below.

Increase Sales

Lighting in Serve-overs

Using the correct type of lighting in your serve-over display will greatly enhance sales. Probably the best is the NAFA light. It is quite expensive, but taken over the year it is only a few pence extra per week. Other types to give consideration to are Philips Colour 32, Atlas Deluxe Natural, and Thorn Deluxe Natural. To do the job properly you should also replace the ceiling lights above the serve-over with one of the above.

Enthusiasm and Knowledge

To increase sales on the delicatessen counter, not only do you need enthusiasm but also enough knowledge to be able to answer most questions. Read all you can about the subject and make a point of going to as many food fairs and exhibitions as possible to see the latest products and to get new ideas on merchandising.

Discounts on New Lines

One way of building the delicatessen sales and establishing whether a new line will sell or not is to ask the supplier for an initial extra discount so that you can give samples to your customers. Tell everyone you have a new line and you would like their opinion about it.

Samples

If you cannot get a special price from the supplier on a new line and you would still like to try it and to give samples, use the following method: Take for example a pie weighing 4lbs that costs you £3.80 and you want to earn 30 per cent POR. First decide how much of the pie you will have to give away as samples in order to sell all of it, remembering that you only give a very small piece as a sample. Perhaps this amount is half a pound. This means that you will have 3½lbs to sell at a gross price of £5.43 (3.80/70 × 100) which equals £1.55 per lb, or 39p per quarter. If the pie sells well and you reorder, you will make 38½ per cent on future sales!

Promotions by Countries

Consider having a two week promotion on the products of one country, not only in the delicatessen cabinet but with 'dry' goods and wines also. If you write to the Tourism Board of the selected country informing them of your proposed idea, they should send you a selection of posters and advertising material.

Filled Rolls

When making filled rolls always leave some of the filling showing. This makes the rolls look far more attractive and enables the customer to make his selection much easier.

Melons, etc.

Extra sales at good profit margins can be made in the summer months by selling ice cold slices of melon. The way to do this is to first place the entire melon on the scale and, by trial and error, work out a selling price per pound in weight to give the required return. Then cut the melon into different sized slices, wrap each in cling film, and price individually on the scale. Display them in the dairy cabinet, and watch your pennies grow!

Economise

Cost of Wrappings

Have you ever priced up your paper bags and wrappings to see how much a pound they cost? Think about it for a few minutes.

Extra Work Surface

If you have a spare chest freezer in your stockroom to take surplus frozen food and ice cream, consider using the top of it as a work surface. All you need is a suitable sized piece of plywood covered in formica which can either rest on top of the freezer or be hinged on the wall so that it falls level with the top.

Bacon

'You never know what you can do until you try.'

One very profitable area of food retailing that is fast becoming a thing of the past, is preparing your own bacon and ham from a complete side. There are very few other products available to the food retailer which can boast the same benefits. What can you think of, for instance, that turns over quickly, has a high unit value, shows over 35 per cent profit (allowing you to undercut the multiples, if you wish), and builds up your reputation locally?

Anyone who can sell 12lb of back and 6lb of streaky a week has sufficient sales to get rid of a whole side of bacon without any trouble. Surely it must be worth 15 minutes of your time per side to gain the above benefits, and into the bargain be selling a top quality product?

Cutting

There are many methods of cutting a side of bacon. The one I recommend is the easiest, and will be described first.

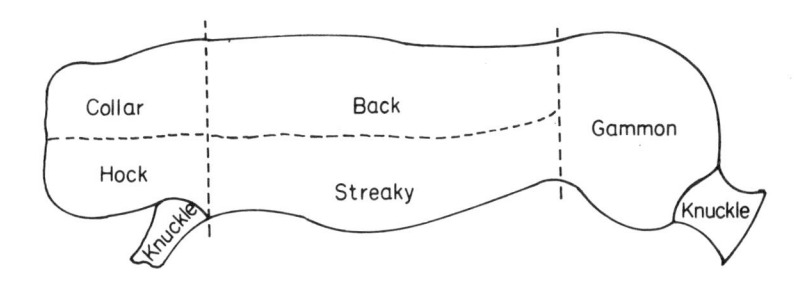

```
┌─────────────────────────────────────────────────────────────┐
│         ╎           ╎                     ╎                 │
│  Collar ╎           ╎    Back             ╎                 │
│         ╎ ──────────┴─────────────────────┤    Gammon       │
│ ────────┤           ╎                     ╎                 │
│   Hock  ╎           ╎   Streaky           ╎                 │
│         ╎Knuckle    ╎                     ╎         Knuckle │
└─────────────────────────────────────────────────────────────┘
```

(1) Make sure all your knives are sharp before you start.
(2) Lay the side on the work surface, back away from you, and wipe it all over with kitchen towel.
(3) Remove the membrane from the rib cage by pulling it off towards you from the spine and discard.
(4) Cut off the surplus bacon from the top of the sternum and put to one side.
(5) Remove the first three ribs from the fore-end individually or in one piece. Keep all bones separately.
(6) Remove any surplus pieces of bone from surface of fore-end.
(7) Lightly cut along both sides and under the end of each rib. Hold the blade of the knife against the rib to keep wastage to a minimum.
(8) Remove the large piece of sternum.
(9) Turn the side around so that the back is now towards you.
(10) Cut approximately one metre of bacon twine and knot the ends together. Double over.
(11) Using one of the rib bones which have already been removed as a handle, pull the string along each rib in turn, freeing it from the meat.
(12) Remove each rib completely, cutting around the small spinal bones with a boning knife.
(13) Cut off and place to one side the piece of bacon over the flat bones in the loin area.
(14) Remove these bones by sliding the knife flat underneath them.
(15) The oyster bone is comprised of two bones, one much larger than the other. Slide the boning knife between them and cut away the smaller triangular piece. Free the meat from the larger bone by pressing down all round it with your thumbs. To remove, push the bone forward until you hear it crack underneath, then cut off with a knife. You will find it easier if you place a cloth over the bone before pushing. This is one of the hardest bones to remove.
(16) Cut out any small bones left on the side.
(17) Run your hand over the side to make sure all the bones have been removed.

(18) The next task is to divide the side into three by cutting off the gammon and fore-end.
(19) Make all cuts at right angles to the back. The gammon is removed by cutting through the oyster indentation. This ensures minimum wastage.
(20) The fore-end is cut off, again at right angles to the back, in line with the fore knuckle elbow bone.
(21) Flatten out the curled piece of flank, and remove the back from the streaky. To determine where to cut place the blade edge of the knife against each end in turn and make a nick in the bacon at a point where the proportion of back and streaky looks correct. Score a line joining the two nicks and cut through.
(22) Cut off the gammon knuckle by following the diagram below.

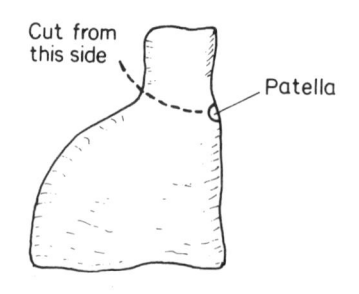

Cut from this side

Patella

(23) Remove patella (knee cap), and free meat from the top of the main leg bone. Then with a gouger push the meat off the bone as far as you can. Cut around ball joint on the other end of the bone and remove.
(24) Cut out triangular aitchbone and remove by pulling off the rest of the sinew attached to the corner.
(25) Trim off excess fat wherever it occurs.
(26) Remove fore knuckle.
(27) Cut off hock by poking finger into the cavity, feeling for the ball joint, and cutting close to this parallel to the collar.
(28) Remove the bone in the same way as the gammon.
(29) Stuff surplus pieces of bacon into the cavity left by the bone.
(30) Rasher approximately half a pound off the fat end of the hock and sell this as bacon pieces. Cut these rashers a little thinner than usual to make them look more.
(31) Tie the hock with three strings and place in a cooking bag.
(32) Tie the gammon tightly with three or four strings and place in another bag.
(33) Twist the ends of the bags and tie tightly.
(34) If you are cooking the collar, remove the rest of the blade bone, and trim off any excess corner fat.
(35) You may cook several pieces of bacon in the same bag.
(36) Cook as per instructions for your ham boiler.

(37) Divide the bones into two equal piles and place in plastic bags. Sell these for 15p–20p each.
(38) Collar may be used as joints, rashers, or for cooking. If used for cooking, remove the blade bone before tying.
(39) Trimming Gammons: think of the finished product; people will not pay top prices for lumps of fat.

Three traditional methods for cutting sides, and variations for the ends. Stages 1–17 as previously described should still be followed in each instance.

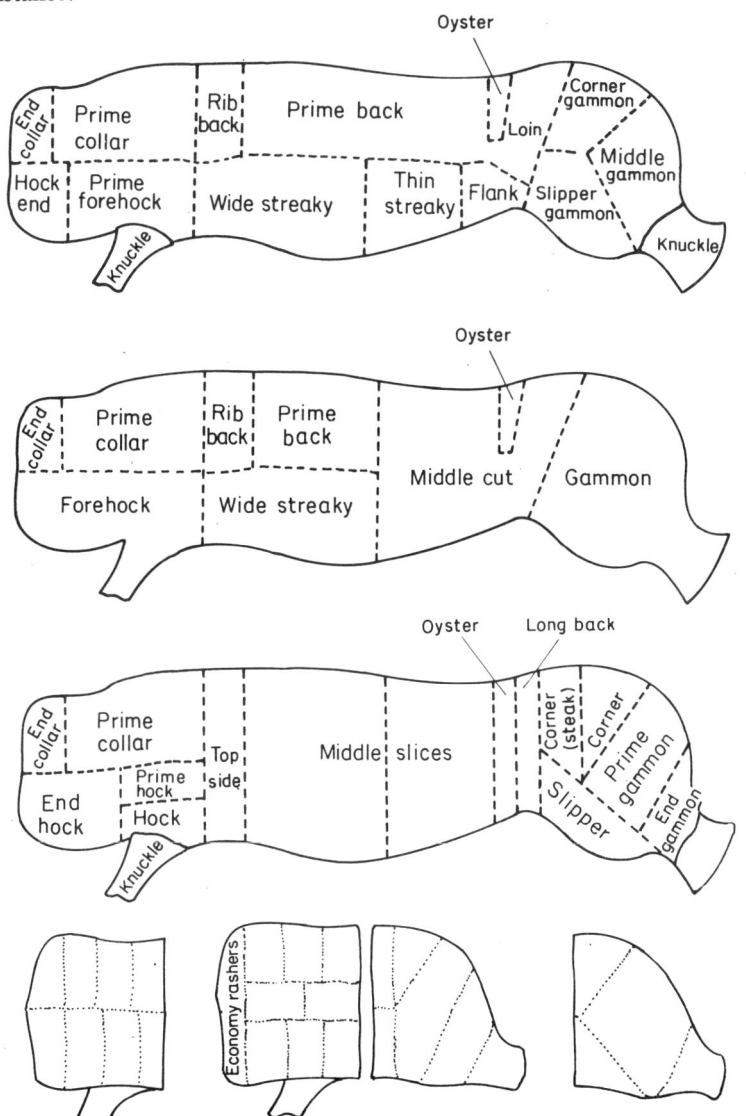

Ways To Sell

There are various ways you can offer the cooked gammon to your customers. For instance, you can finish it off as:

(1) Breaded Gammon. Simply remove the skin and sprinkle golden breadcrumbs all over.
(2) Honey Roast Gammon. Score the rind in a criss cross fashion and brush all over with a mixture of honey and black treacle which has previously been heated. Place in a very hot oven until sufficiently brown, and decorate with slices of pineapple and cherries if desired.
(3) Sugar Cured Gammon. Having boned the gammon put 1lb of brown sugar or 1lb of Golden Syrup all over the meat and leave for 10–12 hours to allow the syrup to work in. Tie it loosely, wrap in greaseproof paper, and leave aside with the rind downwards for another 10–12 hours. Cook normally, still in the greaseproof paper, and allow to set for at least 48 hours after cooking.

THE PROOF OF THE PUDDING!

Side of bacon weighs 63lb @ 70p per lb = £44.10

JOINT	Weight	Price Per lb	Price Per qtr	Amount	Price Per lb	Price Per qtr	Amount	Price Per lb	Price Per qtr	Amount
Back	14	1.60		22.40	1.39		19.46	99		13.86
Streaky	5	95		4.75	79		3.95	59		2.95
Flank	1¾	50		87	50		87	35		61
Collar **	10½	1.96	49	25.48	1.56	39	20.28	1.16	29	15.08
Hock **	6									
End Hock	¾	50		37	50		37	35		26
Gammon **	17	2.64	66	34.32	2.08	52	27.04	1.68	42	21.84
Knuckles	3	Lge 50p	Sm 25p	75			75			75
Bones	1½			30			30			30
Waste/Evapn.	1½									
TOTAL	63			89.24			73.02			55.65
Percentage of profit on return				50.6%			39.6%			20.7%

** The cooked collar and hock is counted as weighing 13lbs after shrinkage, and the gammon is also counted as 13lbs. Losses may not be this great.

In Store Bakeries

'Bread is the staff of life.'

Cost

An in-store bakery can cost between £3,000 and £8,000 + and, if sufficient enthusiasm is put into the venture, it is possible to get your money back in 18 months or so. Profit margins should work out at 30–45 per cent, depending on how much wastage you get.

Depending on your locality it may be possible to increase sales by selling bread to local pubs, hotels, etc., at discount prices.

It is reckoned that you need about £350 sales per week to break even, although you will, in all probability, take more in the rest of the shop, also.

What You Need

(1) You will need a supply of water, a large freezer for storing the frozen products, and possibly 3 phase electricity, depending on the model.
(2) You will also need approximately 100 square feet of sales area to accommodate everything. Nobody has 100 square feet of sales area doing nothing, so equipment and fittings will have to be moved and the chosen area made hygienic. This also costs money. However, this may be a good opportunity to redesign part or all of your shop, bringing in other ideas that you may have had.
(3) Equipment companies usually offer a choice of outright purchase, rental, or hire purchase.
(4) When choosing a product supplier take note of their delivery intervals, because the less frequent these are, the more freezer space you are going to need.

Method

There are three basic methods available:

(1) You can start from scratch with the basic ingredients of flour, water, salt and yeast. There are machines available to do all the hard work for you, such as mixers, etc., but they do make the initial cost higher and are more labour intensive, although they also provide a higher return. It might be better thinking along these lines if sales really take off using one of the other methods.

(2) The most popular method for small shops is using pre-formed frozen dough. The baking equipment consists of a retarder and an oven. Before the bread can be placed in the oven it has to 'prove' in the retarder which means you must still make an early start in the morning if you want to be able to sell bread first thing.

(3) The cheapest way of getting into home baked bread is by using a purely 'bake-off' system. This is where the frozen goods are supplied part baked, and you finish them off in the oven for 10 minutes or so.

Extra Impulse Sales

The smell of freshly baked crusty bread straight from the oven will draw more customers into your shop. Once in, a selection of cakes, including those naughty fresh cream ones, will generate many extra impulse sales.

Fast Foods

'All things come to those who wait.'

'Fast' Foods

Before getting into 'fast food', bear in mind that it may be fast for the customer, but it is definitely not fast for you. It is very labour intensive. Time how long it takes to make a sandwich or a cup of tea or coffee. Because of this, you should not think of the 'catering' side of the business in the same profit margin terms as the rest of the shop. You need to be working on at least 50 per cent profit on return to make it worthwhile, and more on cheaper items that take a long time to prepare such as coffee and tea, so make sure you charge a sufficiently high price for these items. Sixty five per cent profit on return should be the least you are looking at.

Cleanliness

Once you start the fast food business you will have to make sure everything is spotlessly clean, not only for the Health Inspector, but also for the customer, because he does not want to eat or drink something that does not look presentable.

Sandwiches

Would you like to get into the fast food market? Believe it or not, the top selling fast food over the whole country is the sandwich, not the burger.

POPULAR TRADES

Coffee

There is no need to invest in expensive machinery initially, just an ordinary kettle will do. Serve tea and coffee in a 10oz polystyrene cup with a lid. Do not economise on the ingredients, only use top quality brands.

Pot noodles   With that same kettle, you could also sell Pot Noodles. . .

Split packs of sugar   If you build up sales of tea and coffee you will find this an ideal way of getting rid of split packs of sugar.

Soup   If you are selling coffee, you can just as easily sell soup. All you need is the same kettle, the same polystyrene cups, and a packet of 'Cuppa Soup'. Just right for the winter months!

Polystyrene Cups

Polystyrene cups are ideal for hot drinks and soups because they come with tightly fitting lids, they are solid and easy to hold, and because of their insulation properties they keep the liquid inside hot and the outside cool enough to hold with ease.

Hiring Machines

If the soup and coffee trade increases sufficiently (do not forget tea from a tea bag) you may be able to hire a coffee or soup machine from an ingredients supplier at a minimal cost or even free of charge if you guarantee to sell a certain amount of product per month.

Hot Cheeseburgers to Take Away

Several companies now sell ready cooked and frozen cheeseburgers and beefburgers for heating in a microwave oven. They only take a few minutes to heat and prove popular with both teenagers and busy mums.

VAT

Do not forget that you have to charge VAT on ALL hot food and drink that you sell.

Microwaves

'When one door shuts, another opens.'

Domestic Microwaves

If you are selling hot soups, the perfect accompaniment is a microwave oven for heating pies, etc. To start with, or for small quantities, a domestic microwave is sufficient as it will cost only a fraction of the price of a commercial one. However, if trade booms you will need to be thinking of a commercial oven.

Differences

The main difference is that commercial ovens are more robust and are designed for prolonged use. They are also much more powerful, heating foods up to three times as fast. Commercial microwaves start at 1000W (1kW) and are available up to 2kW. The drawback is that they are much more expensive than their domestic counterparts.

Timings

As a rough guide, a 1kW microwave will heat a meat pie in approximately 40 seconds. A 2kW model will take about 20 seconds.

Metal and Foil

Do not place metallic or foil containers in the oven because not only will the microwaves reflect off them, but if damage is done to the machine the manufacturer's guarantee will probably be invalidated.

Paper Cups, etc.

Paper, card, napkins and polystyrene cups can be used in microwaves, but be careful of some of the thin plastics because they might not be able to withstand the high temperatures.

Leakage

Microwave ovens should be checked for leakage by an engineer about every six months, depending on the amount of usage.

Greengrocers

'A Penny saved is a penny gained.'

Fruit and Vegetables

Weight or Number?

There are various regulations concerning the sale of fruit and vegetables. Some must be sold by weight, others by weight or number. The following can only be sold by weight:

POPULAR TRADES

Potatoes	Peas	Cherries	Currants
Beans	Spinach	Blackberries	Mushrooms
Sprouts	Spring Greens	Raspberries	
Brussels tops	Broccoli	Strawberries	

Fruit and vegetables which can be sold by weight OR number are as follows:

Apples	Corn-on-the-cob	Oranges	Shallots
Apricots	Leeks	Parsnips	Swedes
Bananas	Mandarins	Peaches	Tangerines
Beetroot	Nectarines	Pears	Tomatoes
Carrots	Onions	Plums	Turnips

Bunches need not be sold by weight, e.g. carrots, spring onions, turnips, beetroot.

Collections of fruit and vegetables need not be sold by weight, e.g. mixed vegetable packs for a stew.

Display Equipment

Choose display equipment that is easy to fill. This will keep the wastage from low volume sales as low as possible.

Wrapping

Plastic bags should be used in preference to paper bags which are inclined to tear especially when the fruit or vegetables are a little damp. Plastic bags also allow the checkout operator to see the contents of the bag at a glance.

Shop Area Tidy

Try to keep the shop area as clean and tidy as possible. Do not leave empty crates or rotten fruit lying around, and sweep up leaves, etc. whenever you have the chance.

Trim Leaves

Trim off surplus or damaged leaves from lettuce, cabbage and cauliflowers before putting them out for sale.

Bananas

Bananas are best bought underripe, covered loosely with plastic, stored in a cool position, and brought into the shop as needed. Do not put them in a fridge.

Exotic Produce

Exotic produce needs careful handling. Not only must the display look tempting to the customer, but he should also be shown what to do with it.

Self Selection

Loose flow self selection   If you are thinking of going along these lines, the following are some of the pros and cons:

Against

(1) Self selection will not work with large volumes of produce. Displays need to be kept at low volume. This means more work continually topping up.
(2) It is very hard to sell poor quality damaged fruit.
(3) Extra work is needed for tidying up, removing waste, and generally motivating sales by changing positions, special offer tickets, etc.

For

(1) Much more produce is sold on impulse, particularly at busy times, because the customer has much more time to look and choose what he wants, than he would have if he had stood waiting in a queue. There is a lot less pressure on him.
(2) Far fewer staff are needed than for a comparable turnover counter service shop.
(3) The owner of the shop, instead of serving, will be spending most of his time tidying, filling and merchandising the stock. He has much more time, therefore, to be pleasant to the customers and to give advice and suggestions.
(4) Most customers prefer it because they can buy an exact number of items rather than ask for a pound or half a pound of . . .
(5) The indecisive customer will not frustrate the staff nor annoy the customers behind him in the queue. Questions like 'Are they ripe?', 'I think I'll have a few more.', 'No, that's a bit too much. Can you take one off?', 'I wonder if I should buy one for uncle Fred', will all be said in his own time. When he has finally reached a decision, all you need do is price them.
(6) As long as you keep them out of reach of young childrens' fingers, peaches, soft fruit, and other fragile items will not be mutilated and will sell far better on a self selection basis.
(7) Quite often the customer will select produce that you would be reluctant to serve. Most adopt the attitude that he has selected it, and he has only himself to blame. Therefore there are far fewer complaints.
(8) Some people worry about shoplifting with self selection fruit and vege-

tables. Obviously there will be a small amount. This is a by-product of the old maxim 'If they cannot steal it, they will not buy it.' But, looked at realistically, a 50p bar of chocolate could quite easily be concealed, but 5lb of potatoes?. .

Newsagents

*'Early to bed and early to rise
Makes a man healthy, wealthy and wise.'*

Canvassing for New Customers

A large newsbill may bring headaches, but it ensures a healthy profit margin. The backbone of most sizeable newsbills is the morning delivery service. If you are not delivering newspapers, why not start? If you are, why not enlarge your rounds? The solution to both questions is the same. Go out canvassing yourself in the evenings or weekends round the houses you do not deliver to. You have nothing to lose and everything to gain.

Credit A/C's

When you deliver papers you are providing credit to a large number of people, and in order to keep your losses to a minimum you should set a limit to the number of weeks credit you will allow. For bedsitters and other high risk areas think about asking for a week's money in advance.

Paperboys and Papergirls

Age and Hours

It is illegal to employ girls or boys under the age of 13 for paper rounds. It is also illegal for them to start before 7.00a.m.

Morning and Afternoon Deliveries

Have different paper deliverers in the morning to the afternoon, then if one is sick or on holiday you always have a spare you can call on who knows the round.

Holiday Times

At holiday times particularly, keep reminding paperboys to look at the numbers on the papers before delivering them, to prevent strings of houses being given neighbours papers.

Commission

One way of getting new customers for a newspaper delivery round is to pay your paperboys or girls commission for any new business they bring in. They are in an ideal position to do this—all they need do is keep their eyes open for houses changing hands, etc. As a suggestion, you could pay an average week's paper bill as commission, payable after one month.

Increase Profit

Photocopiers

Do you have a photocopier? Are you making full use of it by delivering messages with your newspapers? Details of special offers, clearance sales, new lines, etc. could be circularised every two or three weeks. You could even be paid for it by including customers own paid-up advertisements! If you do not own a photocopier it may be worth your while renting one, or looking round for a secondhand model that carries some form of guarantee.

Greetings Cards

Many displays of greetings cards in newsagents are, to say the least, quite pathetic. They are often dusty and rarely displayed to their best advantage. The average family buys around 30 birthday cards a year. This means that with a catchment area of, for example, 500 houses, there are potential sales of 15,000 cards a year. It must make sense to stock an attractive range of cards, making sure that not only are all the popular relation ones in stock, but that they are also in varied styles to suit all tastes.

Stationery

How about stationery? Many people enclose letters with the cards they send. Why not sell a comprehensive range of writing paper and envelopes, not just the airmail pads and envelopes you so often see.

Video Rental

'Make hay while the sun shines.'

The Future of Videos

Over 55 per cent of UK households currently have a video-recorder. It is predicted that by the end of the century this figure will rise to almost 90 per cent. This is obviously still a fast growing industry.

Questions to Ask

If you are thinking of starting video rentals in your shop, ask the following questions and get the answers in writing before signing any agreements.

Initial Help

What do you get, apart from films, when you start? You should receive a stand, storage cases, promotional advertising, and any necessary bookwork.

Choice of Films

Find out if you can choose your own films. If so, will you have a choice from the new releases as well as from a back catalogue?

Comply with the Law

Make sure the films comply with the Video Recording Act 1984. If they do not you run the risk of a very heavy fine.

Top 50

How many Top 50 films as listed in the national video charts will you receive? You should get at least 30 with every 100 cassettes.

Exchanging

What about exchanging films? How many can be exchanged, how often, and where are they exchanged?

Damage / Loss

What happens about damages to cassettes, or loss? Is there an insurance scheme to protect against this?

Returns Before Lunch

If you ask customers for the top titles to be returned before lunch the following day, you can then rent them out everyday instead of every two days.

Extra Sales From Impulse Lines

Give careful thought as to where your video section is to be sited. Try to get extra sales by placing it near to linked impulse lines such as wines, soft drinks, confectionery and snacks.

Seasonal Fluctuations

Whatever time of year you start your library, bear in mind that generally speaking the winter months are far better than the summer. This means that if you start in the summer and are satisfied with the response, your trade should only grow. If you start in the winter, do not judge a whole year's takings from your present response.

Busy Times

The busiest period of day for hiring videos is generally from 6.00p.m. to 9.00p.m.

Trial periods

If you are approached by a video company and would like to know how video hire would do in your shop, but do not want to commit yourself to a leasing contract or paying out a minimum sum per week, suggest having it on a month's trial and paying them 50p every time a film is hired out during this period. You will soon see in what light the video company regards your location and potential.

Off Licences

'When the wine is in the wit is out.'

Applying for a Licence

Agents

If you are thinking of applying for an off licence, do not be fooled into spending vast sums of money with one of the many companies who say they will handle it all for you at a price. You can probably do just as well on your own. There is no guaranteed way of obtaining a licence, no matter how much you spend.

Newspaper Advertisements

The law states that when you apply for an off licence, you have to place an advertisement saying that you intend to apply 'in a newspaper circulating in the place where the premises to be licensed are situated'. The newspaper does not have to be the one with the largest circulation, nor does it have to be a 'daily'. Weekly newspapers comply with the law. So, if you are applying, and you want as few objections as possible, place your advertisement in the most inconspicuous newspaper you can find. On the other hand, if you have an inkling someone else may be thinking of applying, you will have to keep an eye on each newspaper everyday.

Obtaining an Off Licence

When you apply for a licence, the Licensing Committee will pay particular attention to the following points:

(1) They will need to see that the premises are suitable for the sale of liquor.
(2) They will need to know that you are a fit and proper person to hold a licence.
(3) They will have to be shown that there is a *genuine need* for an off licence.

The Process

(1) Contact your solicitor, find out the dates of the licensing sessions, and decide which date to aim for, bearing in mind all details will have to be with the Clerk to the Justices 21 days before the hearing.
(2) Prepare a plan of the shop showing where the liquor will be displayed and stored. A scale of 1:50 is recommended.
(3) Prepare a map of the area showing ALL licensed premises within at least a quarter of a mile radius. These can be checked at the office of the Clerk to the Licensing Justices from the Licensing Register.
(4) Make up a summary of the location, including type of housing, type of customer, facilities, etc.
(5) Your solicitor will send you a formal notice of application which has to be displayed on your premises prior to the hearing. He will tell you the date on which to display it.
(6) He will also inform the police, local authority, and fire brigade, and you can expect a visit from any of these at any time without prior warning.
(7) Your solicitor will also make sure an announcement is placed in a local paper.
(8) On the day of the hearing you will have to appear in court to answer the magistrates questions.

Protection Orders

If you are buying a business that already has an off licence, remember to apply in good time to the court for a Protection Order to take effect on changeover day, so that you can continue to trade under the existing licence until the next Transfer Sessions, when the licence can be transferred to your own name.

The Law

Licensing Hours

Under the 1988 Licensing Act shops can sell liquor from 8.00a.m. to 11.00p.m. on weekdays, and from noon to 3.00p.m. and from 7.00p.m. to 11.00p.m. on Sundays.

Under Age

Everyone knows that selling alcoholic drinks to persons under 18 years of age is against the law, but did you know that it is also against the law to sell alcohol to anyone *over* 18 if you suspect that it is being purchased for an under 18 year old? Admittedly, this is occasionally very difficult to tell, but usually it is as plain as the proverbial pikestaff. For instance, if you refuse to serve an under age person with three cans of Treble X Gut Rot and a bottle of cider, and two minutes later an elderly person comes in and asks for the same combination, it is perfectly obvious where the drinks are going to end up.

Young Persons

The word 'knowingly' was deliberately dropped from the 1988 Licensing Act. This means that it is no longer necessary for the prosecution to prove that any sale to a person under 18 years old has been made knowingly. It is a defence if you can show that you took all reasonable steps to avoid committing such an offence, or if you had no reason to suspect that the customer was under age.

Staff Under 18

Staff under 18 years of age may only serve liquor if they have written permission from the licensee and if they are also supervised by a person aged 18 years or over. Being supervised means being in the same room. If they are outside the room, even though they are in the same building when the sale is made, the law is being broken. A suggested format for written permission is: 'I . . . ., licensee, authorise . . . ., to sell liquor in my shop whilst a person over 18 years old is present on the premises.'

Drunk

It is against the law to serve anyone who is drunk. You do not *have* to serve anyone you do not wish to, and you do not have to give a reason for refusing to serve. N.B. You must not refuse to serve someone on the grounds of race, religion, or sex.

Drunk Behind the Counter

Did you know that it is an offence for which you can be fined if you are drunk behind your own counter?

Drinking on the Premises

Remember, an *Off Licence* is what it says. It is a licence to sell alcoholic drinks for consumption *off* the premises. If, on a hot day, a customer buys a can of beer from you, walks out of your shop onto the pavement and drinks it, that is perfectly in order, but if he walks out of your door on to your forecourt and drinks it, that is against the law because he is drinking on your premises. The premises are not confined to the shop area but include any land around it, whether forecourt, parking spaces, gardens, etc.

'Low Alcohol' and 'Alcohol-Free'

More and more 'Low Alcohol' and 'Alcohol-Free' beers are being produced, and the Government is trying to persuade us all to drink these, particularly when we are driving. But, how many people know the law regarding sales of these beers? Should they be treated the same as a Top Deck Shandy or Lager and Lime, for instance? The law states that no drink containing more than 1.2 per cent alcohol can be sold to anyone under the age of 18. But it is not as simple as that. This only applies to drinks that have been made specifically up to that proof. If they have been made in the normal beer-making manner and the alcohol then taken out, they are still counted as beer and *cannot* be sold to anyone under age, even though they may contain less alcohol than a can of Top Deck Shandy. Moreover, retailers *still* need a licence to sell these 'Alcohol-Free' beers. The penalty for breaking this law is a fine of up to £1,000. There are moves afoot to update this piece of legislation. You are advised to check with your local licensing authority to find out the current position.

Cider

Cider *is* alcoholic, and a licence is needed to sell it.

Selling Wholesale

If you do not hold a licence, you can still sell wines, spirits and beers on a 'wholesale' basis. You do not need a licence for this. *Wholesale* does not apply to the type of customer you serve, but to the quantity of alcoholic drinks you sell. The minimum for this is: wines and spirits 9 litres, or a full case of 12 bottles containing between 68cl and 80cl; beer and cider 21 litres or two standard cases. You can sell mixed cases of wine, mixed cases of spirits, and mixed cases of beer or cider. You must not have any individual bottles or cans on display.

The law was amended in the Licensing (Retail Sales) Act 1988 to make it legal for these sales to take place *only* from a permanent address. It is unlawful therefore to sell by wholesale quantities from markets or off the back of lorries unless a Justice Licence has first been obtained.

Alcohol By Volume/Original Gravity/Proof

There has been much confusion over the manner in which the alcoholic content of beers, wines and spirits has been expressed over the years, both in this country and abroad. Under an EEC ruling, all EEC countries should have adapted to a uniform system before May 1988, but this has been postponed until May 1989. From that date all alcoholic drinks will have their percentage of alcohol by volume printed on them. As a rough guide;

(a) Beers will contain about 3½ per cent alcohol by volume.
(b) Wines will contain about 11 per cent alcohol by volume.
(c) Sherry/Vermouth will contain about 18–20 per cent alcohol by volume.
(d) Spirits will contain about 40 per cent alcohol by volume.

The *original gravity* of beer is not always an accurate description of the amount of alcohol in the finished product. It is taken after all the ingredients have been mixed together, but before it has been fermented, the usual gravity being approximately 1,035. The gravity of water is 1,000. The amount of excise duty is calculated on this figure and will continue to be done so. As a very rough guide to the amount of alcohol, take the last two digits and place a point between them. Thus an original gravity of 1,084 is roughly equal to 8.4 per cent alcohol by volume. This is, of course, 8.4 parts per 100.

Proof is another description that used to be applied to alcohol, and still is in various parts of the world. 'Proof' spirit contained about 57 per cent alcohol by volume, so roughly speaking 1° proof is equal to 0.57 per cent alcohol, therefore 70° proof is equal to 40 per cent of alcohol by volume, and 120° proof is about 68.4 per cent alcohol by volume. Originally 'proof' was tested by pouring the liquid on to gunpowder and setting light to it. If the gunpowder was dry enough to burn once the alcohol had burnt away, the liquid had been 'proved'.

Displaying Wines

Two of the most common methods of grouping white wines on display shelves are by country of origin or by price. There is a third, however, which makes life much easier for customers who wish to make their own selection, and also gives staff the confidence to advise them. This method is by giving each wine a number from one to eight according to its degree of sweetness (eight being the sweetest) and arranging them accordingly. Suggested numbers for popular wines are:

Muscadet (1)	Piesporter (4)	Moselle (4)	Niersteiner (5)
Graves (2)	B.Bernkastel (4)	Hock (5)	Spumante (7)
Frascati (2)	Entre Deux Mers (4)	Blue Nun (5)	Sauternes (8)
Soave (2)	Le Piat D'or (5)	Liebfraumilch (5)	Premieres Cote de Bordeaux (8)

Christmas Insurance

Check that you are insured for whatever amount of extra stock you will be carrying at Christmas. Most insurance companies automatically increase the cover at this time of the year, but it may still not be enough.

CHAPTER 6

Refrigeration

'Cast not a clout till May be out.'

Freezer Displays

One of the most neglected sectors of the average grocery shop is the frozen food display. This is quite understandable when one considers the difficulties of trying to keep a comprehensive selection of food in a confined space. If you are having difficulties, or you feel you are not selling as much frozen food as you could, try putting the following plan into action. This will take some time and effort initially, but once you have everything planned, not only will ordering and putting away the stock take half the time, but you should not run out of lines, and you should soon see an increase in sales. The first thing you need do is to determine how much space is to be allocated to each section. A suggested layout is shown below:

Cakes Ice-cream Desserts 10%	Fish 20%	Pizzas Pies Pastry 10%	Ready cooked meals 25%	Burgers Chickens Joints etc. 15%	Vegetables 20%

⟵ Traffic flow

Measure the space available in each section and decide on the number of lines that will fit into each. It may take a couple of weeks to get it right. As soon as you are satisfied, take a photograph for future reference. Make out your own order sheet similar to the one below, listing only the lines you are stocking.

REFRIGERATION

B.E. Peas 8oz	20741	/												
B.E. Peas 16oz	20742	/	/	/										
B.E. Petit Pois	20757	/		/										

After a couple of months review the situation by looking at the sales from each section and adjust the spacing accordingly.

British Standards

Before buying a freezer make sure it conforms to either British Standard 3053 or ISO 015 5160 PT11. A cheap model that does not conform to either of these standards will probably not last as long and will probably cost more in maintenance charges, regardless of what the salesman tells you.

Open/Closed Freezers

Closed freezers (those with insulated doors or sliding lids) have lower running costs, but sales from these cabinets are not as high as those from open topped refrigeration.

Wall Freezers

If space is at a premium, consider glass fronted wall cabinets. They are more expensive to buy and run, and sales from them are not as high as from an island cabinet, but they do take up a lot less floor space.

Reserve Stock

If you have the space it is always worthwhile to invest in a chest freezer in your store room either for reserve stock, or to preserve a build up of the fresh foods such as bacon, sausages, cooked meats, etc. This freezer should be able to maintain a temperature of $-18°C$ or colder for foods, and $-21°C$ for ice-cream.

Tidiness

One area that will always need attention is the frozen food display. I will never understand why, after you have spent half an hour or so straightening out the packets and making sure everything is on display, the first customer who comes along wonders what is hidden underneath and immediately dives in and throws the packets all over the place looking for buried treasure. The frozen food section is unique in that it is not absolutely essential to rotate stock in the cabinet each delivery (i.e. put the old on top of the new) because some customers will invariably do this for you. Just watch to see how many take the one from the bottom because it is colder. Little do they know that it is also probably older!

Freezing Food

Putting Away Frozen Food

Make sure you put away your frozen food delivery as soon as possible, especially in the summer. Start by sorting out the ice-cream, mousses, cakes, etc., then the fish, then the meat. Leave the vegetables until last because they have the best resistance.

Freezing Unfrozen Foods

Unfrozen foods should not be put into a sales freezer because of the detrimental effect they have on foods which are already frozen. If you have no option, try to clear a space for them so that they do not touch other foods. The effect on a 5lb bag of frozen chips might not be too bad, but can you imagine what a strawberry mousse would look like?

Ice-cream In Freezers

Try not to keep ice-cream in the frozen food cabinet. These cabinets usually have a temperature of around −15°C. Ice-cream should be kept at approximately −20°C. If there is no other way, keep the ice-cream levels as low as possible in the freezer—no more than two high in the summer. If the quantity of sales make this small amount impracticable, then you will have to invest in a separate ice-cream display case which has been designed to maintain the correct temperature.

Non-Frozen Foods

Never put non-frozen foods in the freezer together with ice-cream because the temperature of the ice-cream will be raised too much.

Keep Cabinets Topped Up

Ice-cream freezers should be topped up early in March regardless of what the weather is like. We quite often have a very hot spell during March or April which then encourages retailers to fill their cabinets after they have lost initial sales. Make sure you are in a position to take advantage of any break in the weather by stocking up early.

Load Lines

Do not fill your freezer above the load line. In fact during a hot summer it is best to try to keep well below this line.

Last Look At Night

Before locking up at night take a last look round the freezers to make sure one of your customers has not left a frozen portion of fish, for example, on

REFRIGERATION

the side of the freezer or on the shelf above. Look to see the level of the food inside the cabinet also, as some customers have a habit of building a tall tower of food well above the load line.

Price Lists

If you stock frozen food from a variety of manufacturers you will find it easier to make up your own price list for use by the checkout or for display purposes by the freezer. All you need do is list the actual goods you stock under the manufacturer's name, leaving a few empty spaces for new lines, and then photocopy several copies. When price increases occur, all you need do is bring a spare sheet up to date.

Maintenance of Freezers

Temperatures

Check your freezer temperatures regularly. If you place a thermometer between the packs of food it should not read warmer than $-15\,°C$ in normal conditions or $-12\,°C$ after a defrost.

Defrost cycle Check the defrost cycle is correct. It should prevent a build up of ice and still keep the top layer of food frozen.

Ice-cream The temperature in an ice-cream cabinet should never be above $-2.3\,°C\,(28\,°F)$. If the temperature of ice-cream has risen above this level it should never be offered for sale.

Hot Air

When siting freezers and chillers, make sure they do not blow hot air into each other. A single unit usually needs some space between it and the wall, and sufficient room above, particularly in the case of chillers, for the hot air to escape.

Hot Weather

Hot weather really increases the workload of freezers and chillers. As the temperature rises the motor has to work harder and harder, and it pumps more and more heat into the shop, which only makes the temperature rise higher, and the motor work harder, and so on . . . The cooler you can keep the shop, the less will be your electricity bill, and the longer your equipment will last. The easiest way of doing this is to create a through draught in the shop by leaving the front door open, and then opening a rear door or window. This is not much use if you have open freezers or chillers along the path of the draught because the cold air will be scooped out of the freezer and replaced by warm air from outside. A steady draught by a freezer will add 30 per cent to your running costs. Shop blinds help a great deal. If you are not able to create a satisfactory through draught, consider having one or more fans set into an outside wall to draw the air out of the shop.

Fans and Freezers

Many of these fans are reversible. They will either pull outside air into the shop or expel it from the shop. Again, be careful where these are sited because if one is placed opposite a freezer and set to draw air into the shop, it will scoop out the cold air from your freezer in no time at all, and you will have a lot of thawed out frozen food on your hands.

Sunlight

As well as keeping the freezer free from draughts you should also make sure it does not receive any direct sunlight. This again can disrupt the temperature of the frozen food. It may be necessary to use window blinds at certain times of the day.

Defrosting Freezers

Watch your freezers carefully for any build-up of ice, even if they are self-defrosting, and dispose of these build-ups regularly. If you do not, you will have less room in the freezer to display goods, it will become less efficient and more expensive to run, and will not encourage customers to buy.

Cleaning

On fridges and freezers the grill in front of the motor should be kept free of dust and rubbish. This is important because the fan behind the grill draws in outside air to cool the compressor and stop it overheating. It is the same sort of principle as cooling a car engine. Do not imagine that because it is producing cold air it does not need cooling!

Night Covers

Covering the tops of freezers and dairy cabinets at night will save on electricity costs. It will not save as much as some salesmen would have you believe, however, because as the outside temperature drops at night anyway, the motor will not be working anywhere near as much as during the day.

Switching Off At Night

Do not be tempted to turn off the freezer at night to save electricity. Not only will this ruin some of the frozen food but it will take a great deal of electricity the following morning to lower the temperature to the correct level again.

REFRIGERATION

Breakdowns

If the cabinet develops a fault or there is a power breakdown, cover the ice-cream with plenty of cardboard and keep the cabinet closed. It should then be alright for about six hours.

Chilled Cabinets

Correct Temperatures

If you are thinking of buying a chilled cabinet, either dairy display or serve-over, make sure the temperature range is correct for the type of products you want to display. Temperature ranges for various groups of foods are as follows:

0°C – 7°C   Cooked meats, butter, margarine, most hard cheeses, and fruit and vegetables apart from melons, bananas, tomatoes, cucumbers and peppers.

0°C – 5°C   Milk, cream, yoghurts, prepared salads, pizzas, most dairy produce, and anything containing fresh or artificial cream.

– 1°C to + 1°C   Fresh meat, minced meat, offal, poultry, fish, and sausages.

Selection In Chilled Cabinets

The chilled cabinet is another area where thought is needed to get the most from a limited space. Be drastic, reduce all slow selling lines to one facing (you will not be continually stocking up because they are slow sellers) or if they are very slow consider not stocking them at all. Fill your new found spaces with fresh lines. If you still do not have enough room, remove everything that it is not necessary to chill such as fruit juices, etc. If you have a vacuum packer you can include a few bulk lines, e.g. one or two pounds of luncheon meat, etc., and even make up some composite packs of your own choice, such as six slices of luncheon meat and three slices of ham in the same pack.

Displaying

It is not the length of refrigerated display cabinet that governs the sales, but the amount of product in it. More sales will be achieved from a well stocked and well presented four foot cabinet than from an eight foot run with the same quantity of foods spread out.

Pre-packed cooked meats   These should either be displayed on hooks at the top of the dairy cabinet, or placed flat on one of the bottom shelves.

Glass Counters

Keep an eye on glass display counters to make sure they are clean and sparkling. It may not be the best of jobs to clear off the remains of a five year old's snotty nose from the front glass, but if it puts you off, just think what it does for the customer!

Chilled Foods

Most people realise the importance of getting the frozen food delivery into the freezer as quickly as possible, but few pay the same sort of attention to chilled foods; yet if these are left lying around for some considerable time before being placed in the chilled cabinet, the results could be just as disastrous. This is particularly true of products that do not contain preservatives. To illustrate the problem, just think how long it would take an ice cube to melt in a warm shop, and then how much longer it would take to freeze again. So it is with chilled products. Just half an hour on the shop floor would need approximately three hours in the cold room to bring the temperature back down to 5°C. An hour on the floor could lead to a 9°C rise in temperature, or even more if left in front of the chiller where warm air is blown on to it. In fact, under ideal conditions bacteria can multiply by dividing into two every 20 minutes. This means that one bacterium could multiply to over one thousand million in just 10 hours! Keep your chilled products fresh—if you cannot find time to display them in the cabinet immediately, store them in your cold room until you do find time.

Check Dates and Temperature Daily

The cabinet should be checked each day for out of date codes and also to see that it is working properly. The recommended temperature of general purpose cabinets is 40°F.

Check 'Sell By' Dates On Delivery

Always check the 'sell by' dates on goods when they are delivered, and if you think they are too short, tell the supplier at once, so that you can get them changed over or at least get an agreement to take back whatever does not sell. You may also be offered a price reduction in order to sell them off cheaper.

Fridge Temperatures

Do you ever wonder how the temperature fluctuates in your dairy cabinet/fridge, etc? All refrigeration finds it hard to cope in the summer, and if your cabinet is not working at its optimum your stock will not last as long as it should. One way of keeping tabs on the efficiency of your refrigeration is to use a 'high/low' thermometer which will record the

REFRIGERATION

highest and lowest temperatures reached. These can be bought quite cheaply, or if you already have one, perhaps in a greenhouse, you could use that.

Dairy Cabinets—Higher Profit Margin

Dairy cabinets are expensive to buy and expensive to run; you are probably talking in the region of £500 per year per metre, but they do have many advantages, the first of which is a much higher profit margin per unit than ordinary grocery lines.

Greater stock turn Chilled products sell much faster than ordinary grocery lines—probably five or six times as fast so you do not need as much money tied up in stock. Higher margins plus less stockholding means larger profits.

Fresh food image The dairy cabinet needs to be well lit, colourful, and tidy to attract customers. If it is sited near to a traditional serve-over both will benefit because your fresh food image will be enhanced. The 'fresh food' image is the area where the real growth in the food market lies.

Health foods There is a growing market for 'health' foods such as cottage cheese, yoghurt and salads, and low calorie desserts. Take advantage of this by keeping a selection in the chilled cabinet.

Back-up Fridges

A cold room, or separate form of refrigeration is very useful for storing fresh products until any short-dated goods have been sold.

Switching Off Serve-overs At Night

There are three advantages in removing all the food from a serve-over and placing it into a cold room when you close at night. The first is the savings on electricity when you switch off the serve-over. The second is the fact that there will not be a build-up of ice in the cabinet, which will make it perform more efficiently, and the third is that you have the opportunity to look at everything when you pack it back the following morning, and of keeping the customers' interest by varying the display from day to day.

CHAPTER 7

Staff

'Many hands make light work.'

Engaging Staff

Value of Staff

Look upon your staff as a capital investment. Taken over a 10 year period, part-time staff will probably cost you at least £25,000, and full-time staff at least £55,000 each! Think carefully about who you employ and whether or not you actually need anyone extra before committing yourself to paying these amounts.

What Type of Person

A happy shop encourages customers to come in and spend their money. Bear this in mind when engaging staff and ask yourself the following questions! 'Will he fit in with existing staff?' 'Will I be able to work with him everyday without being driven round the twist?' 'Will he get on with our existing customers?' 'Is he capable of doing the work?' If you do not have 'yes' to each of these questions, you will be heading for trouble!

Interviews

When interviewing staff always ask questions such as 'What will happen during school holidays, or if the children are sick?' 'Will you be able to work extra hours at short notice if necessary?' 'Did you complete the application form yourself?' (It is amazing how many people cannot read or write.)

STAFF

Tests

If a member of staff is to be employed to handle money, include a simple maths test in the interview. An easy way of doing this is to get him to complete a test at the time of filling in an application form for the job. It does not matter that you have electronic tills and digital scales, there are still occasions when the old grey matter has to be used.

Appraisal

After a member of staff has been working for you for a week, spend a little time going through each of his duties with him, picking out areas where you feel some sort of improvement can be made, and generally telling him how he is getting on. Do it again at the end of the month and ask if he has any suggestions himself. Staff like to be involved and told when they have done something correctly.

Notice Board

When you employ several staff it is sometimes difficult to remember which ones you have told certain things to. If this is the case it may be worth having a notice board in the stockroom, for example, with any relevant messages pinned up.

Staff Management

Smile and 'Thank You'

Encourage staff, by your own example, to greet each customer with a smile, and to say 'thank you'.

Uniforms—Staff Choice

Before making a decision on the type of uniform for staff, give them the chance to express their opinions on the design, colour and type. If you can come to an agreement on the matter it will lead to a healthier relationship between you, and may also encourage them to take better care of the uniform.

Staff's Suspicions

Take staff into your confidence and encourage them to tell you if they see anything at all suspicious. Explain that you have to make a certain amount of profit to pay all your expenses, including their wages, and by helping you they are actually helping themselves. Explain to staff how hard it is to make a profit anyway. Tell them how small the profit margins are on some products and how expensive your bills are.

Effects of Wastage

Impress on staff the effects of unnecessary wastage and damage to stock by carelessness. For example, do your staff realise that if one item from an outer of 12 has to be thrown away, you will have to sell all of the others just to get your money back? Or, if you buy an item such as a round cutting pie, you could actually demonstrate how much you have to sell, taking into account evaporation, trimmings, pieces falling off, etc., just to get back the amount you have spent with a supplier.

Contingency Plans

It saves a lot of time and possible resentment if contingency plans are drawn up for staff holidays and illness. The easiest way of doing this is to take a sheet of paper and list each member of staff in turn, and beside each work out who will cover for them. Make sure that over the year each person is down for the same number of hours. Once this is done, let everyone have a chance to study and comment on it. Finally, make any necessary amendments and stick it on the wall for whenever it is needed. This system also makes working out extra wages much easier because everyone's additional hours will be listed.

Staff Hours

If you think it may be necessary some time in the future to change the days or hours of a member of staff, it is best to make it perfectly clear at the interview that a certain amount of flexibility may be needed with regard to hours worked. This can save a lot of confusion and annoyance later on.

Time Off

There is no payment for the first three days of sickness, but if a member of staff wants time off work for any reason at all, whether it's sickness or pleasure, life will be a lot smoother if they sort out cover amongst themselves. For instance, if a member of staff wants three hours off one afternoon, he can arrange to swap hours with another member of staff or pay this person himself for covering for him. You must, of course, be told what is going on.

Wages

Cash or Cheque

Payment of wages may be made by cash, cheque or bank credit transfer. There is no legal obligation to pay cash, although of course, it makes sense generally to dispose of it this way rather than incur the double expense of paying the cash into the bank and then writing a cheque. If you wish to pay other than by cash to existing staff it will have to be by negotiation. As far as new staff are concerned, just write a paragraph into the contract stating how wages will be paid.

Wages Council Leaflet

An up-to-date copy of the Wages Council leaflet should be displayed for your staff to look at. Absence of this can lead to prosecution.

Wage Rates

The minimum rate stated in the leaflet must be paid to 21 year olds and over. If you have a visit from a Wages Inspector and he finds you are paying below this figure, you may be fined and will certainly have to pay a lump sum for retrospective shortfalls.

Tax and Insurance

Part-time tax/insurance   It is not the number of hours worked that determines whether or not a part-timer pays tax and insurance, but the amount of the wage.

Payments in lieu of notice   Both income tax and national insurance contributions are deducted if wages are paid during a period of notice, but a payment in lieu of notice is usually tax free, as is a lump sum up to £25,000.

Staff Christmas gifts   Gifts made to employees, for instance at Christmas time, do not have to be declared as wages, and are not therefore subject to income tax from the employee, so long as the value of the gift does not exceed £30. Additionally, up to £30 per head may be spent on a staff Christmas party with no tax deductions.

Security

Reduce Opportunities and Temptations

Try to reduce the opportunities and temptations that present themselves to staff. Although it is no excuse, everyone goes through bad patches now and again, and occasionally the temptation may be too great if the opportunity is there.

Pop Into the Shop At Different Times

Pop into the shop at different times to keep staff on their toes. Do not become predictable.

Train Cameras On Staff Areas

If you have security cameras connected to a video-recorder alter the camera angle occasionally before you leave the shop so that you can see exactly what the staff are doing when you are not there. Let them know later what you have seen.

Unusual Actions

Take note of any unusual actions by staff. An example of this is the member of staff who suddenly offered to put the rubbish out into the dustbin each afternoon, and later, on his way home, collected the goodies that he had concealed there.

Tills

'Open/closed' till drawer Most modern electronic tills can be programmed to operate either with an open cash drawer or only when it is closed. If your till has this facility make sure it only works on the 'closed drawer' programme. This means that the drawer has to be closed after each transaction and something has to be rung up for it to open again. If the drawer remains open there is a temptation for staff to just put the money in the till without ringing it up and later on to pocket this amount of cash.

Till checked everyday It is generally accepted that most shop losses are caused by staff, so make sure your staff know that you check the till everyday. Tell them that everything they do on the till is recorded and is given to you at the end of the day in the till analysis.

Checkout errors Do not allow staff to use the 'minus' button on tills or to correct mistakes themselves. If they make a mistake tell them they must write the amount on a piece of till roll, sign it, and place it in the till. You will take it into account at the end of the day when the till is checked.

Spot checks If you have suspicions of a member of staff, have a spot check on the till for whatever reason you wish. It is a good idea to do this occasionally anyway; it keeps the staff on their toes.

Tills 'over' If you do a spot check on the till and you find the cash is over, be very wary. It could mean that one of the staff has been underringing and has just not had the opportunity, or was not ready to take out the cash.

Underringing Take note of coins put into an unusual compartment, or pieces of paper with columns of figures written down. These could be a check of amounts underrung on the till to show the till operator how much to take out when the opportunity arises.

Discuss till discrepancies Always ask the staff about till discrepancies. It proves to them that you do really check the till and should make them more careful.

Staff ringing up own goods Do not let staff ring up their own goods and take their own change, and on no account let them take their wages from the till. It is surprising the number of shopkeepers that do. This is just asking for trouble. Most people in certain circumstances will be tempted to 'take a little extra' meaning to replace it later on. The trouble is 'later on' rarely comes, and having done it once and got away with it, the second time is easier, and the third, and so on. . .

Staff bags Do not allow staff to leave their bags near valuable stock such as cigarettes, spirits, etc., for the same reason as above.

Check staff bags It is sensible to include in the contract of employment a condition stating that you are allowed to check staff bags. If staff come to expect random bag searches the chances of stock theft will be reduced.

Staff/customer collusion Keep an eye open for staff/customer collusion at the till—this usually takes the form of not ringing up all the items or underringing some. Be especially wary if staff serve their own relations.

Taking goods without paying Try not to take goods from the shop, in sight of the staff, without paying for them. This will only encourage them to do the same. If you must do it, explain to the staff that you keep a note of this and account for it all at the end of the week.

Staff responsible for cash shortages If you want to make your staff responsible for cash shortages in the till, or stock shortages, you will need to include this in the contract, or have it agreed to in writing in advance, by the employee. The most you can deduct per week is 10 per cent of the gross pay on a pay day, until the full amount is recovered. The 10 per cent limit does not apply to an employee's final instalment of wages. Therefore, if an employer has not had long enough to recover all that is owing under the rule, he can do so when the employee leaves.

Staff deductions Employers may only make deductions for shortages during the 12 months following the discovery of the shortage. The employer must tell the employee, in writing, the reason for the deductions and the total amount to be held back from his pay.

Educating Your Staff

You can educate and make your staff more proficient by either letting them look through this book or by selecting passages for compulsory reading. Following this you will usually get responses such as 'Oh, I didn't know that', or 'I'll try that next time'. Not only will your staff benefit from improving their knowledge, but they will also generally find it very interesting, and of course, the more proficient *they* become, the more *you* will benefit. For those who do not have enough grey matter to comprehend what it is all about, you will have to explain in your own words.

CHAPTER 8

Security

'When the cat's away, the mice will play.'

Cheques

Cheque Cards

Never accept a cheque for more than £50 with a cheque card believing that at least you will be guaranteed the first £50. The cheque card does not apply to any cheque made out for more than £50.

Two Cheques for Same Transaction

Do not accept two cheques under £50 for the same transaction. If the bank suspects that this has been done, neither will be guaranteed.

Bankers Cards—What To Look For

Make sure staff understand what to look for when accepting a cheque accompanied by a banker's card.

(1) The signature must be the same. Make sure the cheque is signed in front of you. If it has already been signed, ask the customer to sign again on the back of the cheque. If the cheque has been stolen, he may have spent a considerable time practising the signature, but will find it a different matter being asked to sign again quickly. It is a good idea to write his address on the back of the cheque also.
(2) The card must be in date.
(3) The bank codes must agree.
(4) The card number must be written on the back of the cheque by a

member of staff—if it is written by the customer the bank could refuse to honour it. It is a good idea to make staff write the expiry date of the card on the back of the cheque also. This will ensure they look at it.

Stolen Cheques and Cards

If the customer signs the cheque in front of you, and this signature corresponds with that on the cheque card, the bank must honour the cheque, even if both have been stolen. If they have been stolen, and there is a difference in the signatures, you can say goodbye to your money.

If you are not completely satisfied with either the cheque or the person, do not accept it.

If you are suspicious about a cheque card and feeling brave, impound it and take it to your bank—there may be a reward waiting for you! On the other hand there might be a black eye.

A cheque card cannot be used with a cheque drawn on a limited company.

Special Presentation

If, after checking everything thoroughly, a cheque is returned to you marked 'cheque card and cheque book stolen, signature differs', you can make what is called a 'special presentation'. Go to your bank manager and ask him to make a special presentation to the bank on which the cheque is drawn. You will have to write a covering letter stating that all cheque card conditions were met and the cheque was accepted in good faith. Your bank may charge you for this service, so find out first, especially if the cheque is for a small amount.

Single Cheques

Beware of anyone who has a single cheque without a cheque book.

Bounced Cheques—Small Claims

It is a criminal offence to issue a cheque knowing that there are insufficient funds in the account to honour it. If, somehow or another, this happens to you, think very carefully before proceeding with a county court or small claims summons, because you could very easily become more out of pocket. It is not too difficult to get the court to find for you and to agree a set weekly or monthly amount to pay, but you should realise that the likelihood of receiving one penny of it is very remote. Even if you pay extra for a bailiff to attend, you will probably receive a report something like 'nothing of value'. This probably means that the customer does not actually own anything—everything is either rented or on hire purchase, and probably about to be reclaimed by someone else.

Tills

Make sure you empty the till of notes regularly. You are only asking for trouble if you leave the drawer bulging with wads of notes. Some people will not be able to resist the temptation.

Tills Open At Night

Always leave your till drawers open at night, after taking out the insert and placing it out of view, particularly if the tills can be seen from the outside of the shop. If you lock the till at night it will only make a thief think there is a quantity of cash inside and he will either smash the till to open it, or steal the whole thing—modern tills are not very heavy!

Floats—Take Out £1's and 50p pieces

If, when you hide the till insert, you leave the following morning's float in it, you should protect yourself further by bagging all £1 coins and 50p pieces and placing them out of sight also. Never leave notes in the till overnight.

Do Not Count Cash Near Windows

Never check the till and count the cash after you close in view of the shop window. There is no point in putting thoughts into people's heads.

Colour Coding Goods

If you wish to separate different classes of goods at the till, either for keeping a tally of certain types of goods, or for identification of standard-rated and zero-rated items, you will find it much easier if you use a separate coloured price ticket for each group. To make it easier still for the cashier, a ticket of the correct colour should be stuck over the appropriate department key on the till; the most used colour to the front.

Change In Pocket

If a certain amount of loose change is kept in a separate pocket of your overall instead of being rung up on the till, you will find it much easier dealing with the odd refund or small overring on the till. In the first instance give the customer a refund from your pocket, and in the second put the money into the till to keep it straight. At the end of the day, or if an excess builds up, ring up the surplus from your pocket in the proportions of your normal trade.

Children

Always look closely at children who are with their parents at the cash desk to see if they are carrying anything. Sometimes they pick up items without their parent's knowledge. Sometimes it is a deliberate method of stealing which is actively encouraged by the parent.

Remove Everything From Baskets

Make sure everything is removed from the customer's basket when ringing up on the till. All too often something small is concealed, not always intentionally, beneath what appears to be the last item to change for.

Underline Ambiguous Prices

To save confusion at the checkout as to whether a price is 69 or 96, 68 or 89, 16 or 91, etc., make sure you underline the correct price when writing on bags and packets, e.g. 9<u>6</u>, 8<u>9</u>, and 1<u>6</u>.

Shoplifting

Customers Stealing

The first, and sometimes hardest thing to realise, is that no matter where your shop is situated, and no matter who your customers are, if stock is displayed in an open manner you will be subjected to stealing, or shoplifting as it is politely called. In every community there will always be an element who try it, whether from need or excitement, and having got away with it once, they will do it again and again. There is, of course, the odd time when someone walks out of the shop inadvertently without paying for their goods. When they see how easy it is, a proportion of these will start on a regular basis. That is the second thing to realise—in most cases, shoplifting is not just an isolated incident. Do not believe your customers are different to others. Give them the chance and they will steal from you just as easily as they will from anyone else, and smile at you into the bargain as they do it. Once you accept this, you have taken your first step towards prevention.

Large Stores Can Afford It

Small shops need to pay far more attention to shop theft than large stores because a much higher percentage of stealing occurs in small shops. Not many people realise this, but it is easy enough to work out. Take the grocery trade as an example. Just assume that out of every 100 customers there is one thief. He can only steal the same amount of goods no matter how large or small the shop is. Say the value of what he steals is £6. The average customer spend in a small shop is probably somewhere in the region of £1.50, so out of 100 customers @ £1.50 (£150) you lose £6, which is four per cent of your turnover. The superstores probably have an average customer spend of over £20, so they lose that same £6 against a turnover of at least £2,000, which is .3 per cent. This means that small shops are losing over 13 times as much stock by comparison, as large ones! No wonder the level of security in most large stores is so small.

Shrinkage

To get the whole thing in perspective, it is generally estimated that shrinkage accounts for somewhere between two per cent and four per cent of turnover. *This is the equivalent of between one and two weeks takings disappearing each year*!

Annual Shrinkage Another way of expressing annual shrinkage losses is to say that if these are between two and four per cent of turnover, that is roughly equivalent to half your total wage bill, if you include your own wages.

Young Males

The majority of shoplifters are young males and most of these are under 21 years old. This means that you will not go far wrong if you look upon every youth with suspicion.

American Statistics

According to American statistics for shoplifting in supermarkets in 1987, shoplifters are more often than not males, most of these between 18–29 years of age, and most are caught between 3.00p.m. and 6.00p.m. It is estimated that the total loss to food orientated retail businesses is more than $200 million a year.

Customer Looking At You

If, every time you look at a customer, he is looking at you, in all probability he is up to no good.

Customers In Twos and Threes

Beware of customers who come in in twos and threes and whilst one of them asks you questions and keeps you occupied the others wander off aimlessly and fill their pockets.

Children In Pairs

Many shops have signs such as 'No more than two unaccompanied children at any one time'. If you are having problems with schoolchildren consider doing this.

Customers Without Baskets

If you see any customer walking round carrying goods in his hands, offer him a basket, saying that not only will he find it easier, but that you also get less breakages. If he is not trying to steal he will thank you for it; if he is trying to steal, he will realise you are watching him.

Customers Eating In Shop

Try to notice, whenever possible, what people are carrying when they come into your shop. This is a help if they approach the checkout eating an apple, or a bar of chocolate, or a packet of crisps. The simplest answer to this problem is to automatically charge for anything you see them eating. They will soon tell you if they bought it elsewhere, and they may learn not to buy goods somewhere else and eat them in your shop.

Damaged Goods

Watch out for customers damaging boxes of goods and then asking for reduced prices.

Thieves—Quiet Times In Shop

Do not believe that the more people you have in a shop the more likely you are to have goods stolen. Thieves do not like to be noticed and are in their element at quiet times in the shop when there are few customers around, and the staff are preoccupied chatting, or filling the shelves.

Apprehending Customers

There are many shopkeepers, probably far more than will admit to it, who are apprehensive about challenging someone they feel sure is stealing, because of the possible consequences. 'Will they become violent?', 'Will their friends and relations boycott the shop?', 'If the police are involved, will it mean having to take time off to go to court?' All these and more flash through the mind, yet the most important question will have to be put there conciously by you, and that is, 'Can I afford *not* to do anything?' The plain truth is that if they get away with it, not only will they continue stealing from you, but they will also tell their friends, who in turn will tell theirs. . . Regardless of the reason you give for running a shop, the most important one is to make a profit. If you do not make a profit, you go broke.

Method of Three

If you suspect someone of stealing, try using the 'method of three' to catch him. This is a quick and simple method of checking to see if anything has been removed from a shelf. All you have to do is to take a box or self service basket and remove sufficient items so that each susceptible line left on the shelf is divisible by three. The shelves will look completely natural and may be easily checked in seconds.

Password

It is a good idea to have a password to make a member of staff watch someone. This should be something quite innocuous, such as 'Have you seen the Cadbury rep recently?'

Adding Cost of Stolen Goods to Bill

If you see someone stealing something and you do not want the aggravation of confrontation and accusation, a simple method is to either deliberately overcharge him, or if you know exactly what he has taken to ring up that amount. If he disagrees with the total you are asking for, he will have to take out the goods he has purchased for checking purposes, at which point you can say about the pot of . . . you saw him putting in his pocket. If he says nothing in the shop, but checks his goods when he gets home, he will see that he has been charged for what he has stolen and will realise he has been watched, and probably think himself lucky he has not been prosecuted.

Proof of Shoplifting Beyond Reasonable Doubt

If you find after security checks that you have been losing, for example, a tin of salmon or a packet of scampi each day for two weeks, and you set a trap and catch the thief, you will only be able to prosecute for the one theft because you will not be able to prove that past losses were due to the same person beyond reasonable doubt. Remember, the accused is completely innocent of everything until proved guilty, and then he is only guilty of that which can be proved.

Watch New Faces

If you think, after taking every precaution you can imagine, that you have almost succeeded in stamping out shoplifting, do not get complacent. New people move in and out of areas all the time, and your next resident may be a bigger villain than any you have had in the past.

Right of Refusal

Remember, your shop is private property and you have the right to refuse entry to anyone you want without giving an explanation. Your shop is not a public place, and the public have no rights whatsoever to come in if you do not want them to.

Deterrents

The main way of reducing shoplifting is to show your customers that the only certainty in life is that anyone who steals from you will eventually be caught.

SECURITY

Small Goods

Small valuable goods should be displayed out of reach of the customer, accessible only to a shop assistant.

Small Bottles of Spirits

Never allow customers to touch half, quarter, eighth or miniature bottles of spirits until they have paid for them, even if it means taking the money separately from the rest of the shopping.

Ticketing

Using a pricing system peculiar to your shop stops the customer saying that he bought an item 'down the road'. (This is yet another reason for using the dating system suggested on page 22.)

Displaying Photographs of Stealing

Make it known as widely as possible when you catch someone stealing. If you have them on video tape, you can take a photograph off the television screen and stick that in a prominent place in the shop. This has far more effect than anything else. (See page 137 for law on photographs.)

Cameras

Cameras covering checkout A video camera and recorder trained on the till has the dual benefit of being able to see exactly what each customer is paying for and how much has actually been rung up on the till. It stops the customer saying he has paid for it already and it keeps staff on their toes. An added benefit is that it stops a customer coming back to say that he gave a £5 note and only received change from £1. If the tape is replayed, everything purchased will be seen, the money tendered will be shown, and also the position in the till where the cash was placed.

Hidden camera If you really want to find out about your customers and staff, train a *hidden* video camera connected to a video-recorder on a danger area and leave it recording all day. You will soon find out who your friends really are.

Size of monitor As far as monitors for closed circuit television are concerned, the larger the better. Small screens are useless because you cannot make out anything on them. Large screens draw people's attention and are much more of a deterrent.

Be Alert

Be alert at all times in the shop. The more security equipment you have—mirrors, cameras, etc., the more alert you should be because the more you have to look at.

Compare Amount Stolen with Net Profit for Half a Day

Do not take shoplifting lightly. Many shopkeepers mentally compare the amount stolen against their turnover, and are not too bothered. This is wrong. Take for example a shop taking £2,000 per week. If £5 worth of goods are stolen, they tend to compare £5 with £2,000, which is obviously a very small amount. What they should compare it with is their *net* income for that morning, which will probably be in the region of £15. That £5 in reality represents one third of their profit for that morning!

Credit Information Agencies

If you want to find out what sort of credit rating you have, and what information would be passed on to a company enquiring about you, write to either or both of the following credit information agencies who will tell you what fee they require, and upon receipt of this sum they will send you the same information that they pass out to their members:

UAPT INFOLINK, Regency House, 38 Whitworth Street, Manchester, M60 1QH, or
UAPT INFOLINK, Zodiac House, 163 London Rd., Croydon, CR9 2RP., 6865644.
CCN SYSTEMS LTD, Lincoln Chambers, Lincoln St., Nottingham, NG1 3DJ.

Small Claims Fees

If you decide to use the small claims service to recover debts you will have to pay the court fees in advance. These are approximately 10p for every £1 claimed, with a minimum of £7. This amount is added to the debt, and in theory at least, will eventually cost you nothing. But, if you think there is no likelihood of the debt ever being repaid, it is just throwing good money after bad, unless you want the self-satisfaction of causing as much trouble as possible for the so-and-so's.

Shop Premises

Vulnerability

Is your shop safe? Do you know where a burglar would try to gain entry? The easiest way to find out is to walk round the outside of your shop imagining yourself to be locked out, bearing in mind that most burglars will be quite nimble and not afraid of heights! And do not delude yourself into thinking that they will not want to make a noise. Most professionals will break something far quieter than you would, and even if a neighbour does hear something, the odds are that he will do nothing about it because in all probability he will not want to get involved.

Flat Roofs

Flat roofs are a favourite point of entry. Look to see how easy it is to get on to your flat roof, and once there, how vulnerable it is. It is sometimes easier and more effective to protect these areas by alarms or floodlights from outside.

Drainpipes

Drainpipes can have barbed wire tied round them.

Windows

Having found out the weak spots you now need to make them safe. Windows should have proper locks fitted, and should not be left with just a catch which can easily be undone by smashing the glass. Those that are not used should be screwed up (metal frames can have coach bolts through them, or even be welded). Grills or bars should be fitted over them where convenient.

Laminated Glass

If you are having a new shopfront installed, or are replacing one of your windows, ask for laminated glass. It is slightly more expensive than ordinary 6mm glass, but has the advantage that if a brick is thrown at it, it will only crack or craze, but will not fall apart. To make a large hole in it you will need to stand there thumping away with a hammer for some considerable time. If it only has a couple of cracks you will not need to board up. If the damage is more extensive, the boarding-up procedure is much simpler than with ordinary glass and much safer.

Skylights

Skylights should be treated in the same manner as windows with grills or bars fitted underneath them. If skylights are not essential, give serious consideration to doing away with them altogether.

Doors

Weak doors should be replaced with solid hardwood at least two inches thick. Steel doors, or steel lined doors are even better. Make a point of always locking interior doors to slow down anyone who does happen to get in.

Locks Bolt doors whenever possible and make sure that locks are of the five lever deadlock mortice type with a one inch throw into the frame. On no account rely on cheap or Yale-type locks as these can be opened with the minimum of effort.

Door Frames Pay particular attention to door frames. If these can move so can the actual doors, regardless of what they are made from, how strong they are, and what locking devices are used. Doors should fit snugly into their frames. If they do not, they can easily be jemmied open.

Hinges Hinges should always be fitted inside the door. If they are on the outside it only needs the central pin to be knocked out, and the door can be lifted off. If you have no alternative but to fit them outside, you should use hinge bolts or ordinary bolts on the hinged side of the door as well as on the opening side.

Letter Boxes

Letter boxes should only just be large enough to receive the post. Many break-ins have occurred when boxes are large enough for hands, arms, or even hooks to be slid through and bolts withdrawn and locks undone. A bottomless box fitted to the inside of the door will provide a useful deterrent.

Dark Spots

Take a look at night to see if there are any unlit spots near doors and windows where a burglar could be concealed whilst breaking in. If there are, have exterior vandal-proof floodlighting fixed, and do not forget to turn it on at night.

Fingerprints

Clean your window sills regularly. This makes it much easier for the police to find fingerprints if you do have a break-in.

Reserve Stock In Stockroom

Cigarettes, wines, spirits and other expensive stock—you obviously have to display sufficient lines to give a full selection and to make the shelves look attractive, but do not overdo it—keep your reserve stock in the stockroom out of sight, not piled high behind the counter.

Goods Left Near Doors At Night

Do not put temptation in the way of casual passers-by by leaving anything of value near the door or windows at night. Even dump bins of crisps left within arms reach of a letter box is enough to make some young moron poke a stick through and try to spear a packet. What you do not want is a group of youths standing outside your shop working out the best way of breaking in.

Deterrents

Deterrents for Thieves

Unless you have something very valuable on your premises, the thief will not want to spend too much time breaking in. He will also want to make a quick getaway with your goods. Anything that will slow him down will act as a deterrent.

Getaway Vehicles

If the thief is after bulky or heavy goods he will need a vehicle to take them away. Give thought to this side of it as well, to make things as awkward as possible.

Dogs

As most shops are attacked from the back and at night, one of the best deterrents is a dog. Small yappy ones are the best, such as Pekinese, Yorkshire Terriers and Pugs. Perhaps the best of all is a relatively new and increasingly popular breed called the Shih Tzu (pronounced 'sheed-zoo'). These dogs are also extremely agile and fast. Needless to say, the more dogs you have, the more effective the deterrent.

Alarm System

Alarms—light and noise   Most shop burglaries occur at night. An alarm system that provides floodlighting of the area as well as a loud noise is therefore more desirable.

Burglar alarms   Manufacturers have made giant strides in recent years, and their systems are now very sophisticated, and actually cheaper than they were a few years ago. They are generally activated by movement, body heat, vibration, or noise, and many have the advantage of minimal installation costs. If you decide to fit one yourself, make sure your insurance company will accept it.

Alarms—NSCIA approved   Check also that your alarm company is approved by NSCIA (National Supervisory Council for Intruder Alarms). Many insurance companies insist that they will only recognise systems fitted by NSCIA members. If you want to check whether a company is a member of NSCIA, or you have a complaint, write to: NSCIA, St Ives House, St Ives Road, Maindenhead, Berks.

Crime Prevention

Most shopkeepers think seriously about crime prevention after the event. This is too late. Your aim should be to prevent a burglary happening at all, not to make the next attempt more difficult than the last.

Shop Left Empty

If you do not live above the shop and shut for a few days at Christmas or holiday time, inform the police and ask them to keep an eye on the premises as well as popping over yourself in between times to make sure no catastrophes have happened, e.g. power failures, gas leaks, etc.

Handling Cash

Bank Regularly

Cash should be banked regularly, not only to keep your balance as high as possible, but also, just as importantly, to reduce the risk of loss from burglary in the shop, or being attacked on the way to the bank.

Vary banking times   When going to the bank it is adviseable to vary your days and times as much as possible, so that your movements are not predictable.

Banking in post office (GIRO)   If there is a bank in your parade life is much easier. If not, one way of minimising risks is to use the Post Office National Girobank system if you have a post office nearby.

Safes

If you must keep cash on the premises invest in a reliable safe and have it bolted to the floor, or set in concrete, or permanently fixed and hidden by some other means, and do not forget to hide the key. Your insurance company will advise you on makes of safe.

CHAPTER 9

Bookwork

'It is an undoubted truth, that the less one has to do, the less time one finds to do it in. One yawns, one procrastinates, one can do it when one will, and therefore one seldom does it at all.'
                                        Philip Dormer Stanhope, Earl of Chesterfield
                                        (1694-1773)

Stocktaking

Clear Out Slow Movers

Stocktaking time provides a good opportunity to take a hard look at the proportions and selection of stock and to clear out any extremely slow moving or obsolete lines. Mark down any goods that you think an independent stocktaker would query if you were selling the business. The final figure will then be an accurate one for the opening stock of the following year, and a guide for insurance purposes.

How to Do It Yourself

Professional stocktakers usually charge between one per cent and four per cent of the final value of the stock, i.e. between £70 and £280 for £7,000 worth of stock, although in some instances a set figure may be agreed upon. It is far better financially, and not too difficult if organised properly, to do the stocktake yourself, especially if you are able to call upon several members of the family to help. Use the following method:

(1) Two days before the stocktaking date, remove sufficient stock from your stockroom and put on to the shelves and counters of the actual shop area.

(2) Do not arrange for any stock to be delivered during this two day period. During this time count all the stock in the stockroom.
(3) During the selected day for stocktaking, areas of the shop which are particularly slow moving should have their stock counted whilst the shop is open. Do the rest of the shop after closing time.

Extra help Extra help with counting the stock is essential. Make sure members of your family and staff know in good time when stocktaking is going to occur so there is no excuse for them not to be there.

Stocktake in pairs It is quicker if the stocktake is done in pairs—one person calling out the price and counting the number, the other writing it down.

Stocktaking form Make a plan of the shop and number the different sections. Decide which order you will do them in and complete one sheet for each section. A suggested format is shown below. When you have finished, check each section has been completed.

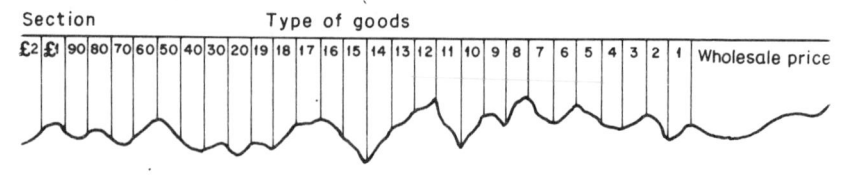

Section										Type of goods																
£2	£1	90	80	70	60	50	40	30	20	19	18	17	16	15	14	13	12	11	10	9	8	7	6	5	4	3	2	1	Wholesale price

Total Retail Value £   Wholesale Value £   Total W/Sle Val. £

Counting in fives and sixes When counting stock it may be beneficial to use one of the following methods:

(1) Counting in fives 1(one), 11(2), 111(3), 1111(4), 1̶1̶1̶1̶(5),
    Therefore: 1̶1̶1̶1̶ 1̶1̶1̶1̶ 1̶1̶1̶1̶ 1(16).
(2) Counting in sixes 1(one) ⌐(2), ⌐│(3) □(4) ⌑(5) ⊠(6)
    Therefore: ⊠ ⊠ ⊠ ⊠ ⌐(26).

Using a calculator If using a calculator make sure you have fresh batteries before you start. Do not total whole walls in one go—if you make a mistake on the calculator you will have to start again, and do not write down the figures automatically without thinking about them just in case you pressed one or two extra '0's by mistake!

Costing Stock may be listed at cost price, at selling price, or a combination of both, but mark each accordingly at the time to save confusion later.

Listing Where possible list at cost price. Keep a few relevant invoices handy for bulk items.

Translate to cost price Translate the value of the stock into one of cost price by reducing selling prices by an estimated gross profit percentage.

Final check Once you have finished, have a final check around the shop for odd corners, shop windows, tops of fittings, etc., to make sure everything has been counted. Do not forget outside the back of the shop for empty crates and bottles.

Stock figure only correct at that time Remember that your stock figure will be accurate only at the time you complete it. It will not necessarily be a typical figure for the rest of the year. A large delivery a few days later will change the amount dramatically.

Tie in VAT quarter to financial year If using a VAT scheme which needs a stock figure you should tie in your VAT quarter to your financial year so that the one stocktake does for both.

Year to year analysis of stock Once you have calculated your stock compare various sections with the figures for last year and the year before and then decide whether you have enough or too much stock for the amount of sales from each section.

Stock levels Knowing what your stock level is at any time of the year is always a grey area. To get a quick approximation of what it should be, you will need to start from last year's accounts. The two figures needed are the closing stock figure and gross profit percentage. First, add up all your purchases since the end of your financial year and add this figure to the stock value shown on the accounts. Next, add up all your sales during the same period and translate this into a cost price by using last year's gross profit percentage. This is simply done on a calculator. For example, if your sales to date are £40,000 and your percentage of profit is 16 per cent, then the calculation would be 40,000 × 84% = 33600. To find your present stock, deduct this figure (cost of sales) from the previous one (stock at year end plus purchases). To make life simpler, and to keep as up to date as possible with your stock position, you should do this as a matter of course after you have finished your weekly accounts when the figures are there before you. As an example, if your closing stock value was £10,500 and your profit margin 16 per cent, your first week's takings £3,400 and your purchases £2,250, the calculation would be as follows:

Cost of Purchases	(£10,500 + £2,250)	= £12,750
Cost of Sales	(£3,400 × 84%)	= £ 2,856
	Present value of stock	£ 9,894

This figure will not take into account stock which has been delivered but not yet paid for. To get this figure, total all unpaid invoices and delivery notes for goods received, and add to your present stock value.

Use your own stocktaker To save time and arguments always employ a stocktaker when buying or selling a business. Never share the cost of a stocktaker with the person you are buying from or selling to. Always use your own stocktaker. It may cost you slightly more in fees but at least at the end of the day you will have peace of mind.

Banking

Asking for Loans

If you are looking for a loan, there is little difference between the major clearing banks. Your contact will be the manager. If you do not think he is particularly interested in your project, try elsewhere.

Have all the information ready   When you approach your bank manager for a loan, make sure you have all the information you need written down in a legible form. You will need to know how much you need to borrow and how much you can afford to repay per annum, and most importantly, you will have to show where this money is coming from, taking into account all your additional expenses.

First impressions count   Present the whole package to the bank manager neatly in a folder. First impressions count, and you cannot do better than getting off to a flying start.

Interest   Interest payable on loans and overdrafts is usually linked to the base rate. A 'fixed rate' loan means the base rate will stay the same throughout the period of the loan. If the loan moves up and down with the base rate it is called a 'floating' rate. Unless absolutely necessary, do not agree to any higher figure than base rate plus three per cent.

Writing Cheques

When writing cheques always start both your words and figures as far to the left as possible in order to prevent possible fraud. To show how easy this is to do, look at the examples below of an actual cheque received by me.

A/C payee only   It is better to be safe than sorry. For an extra five seconds you can be certain that if a cheque you have posted goes astray, it will not be cashed by anyone else. All you need do is write 'A/C Payee Only' on every cheque you write as a matter of course. If the cheque is stolen, you will not be out of pocket.

A/C payee only—cashing   If someone asks you to cash a cheque for them, and it has 'A/C Payee only' stamped across it, do not cash it. In all probability the cheque will be returned to you and you will be charged about £2.50 for it. That is unless your surname is the same as the payee on the cheque!

Cheques—'not negotiable'   'Not negotiable' written on a cheque does not mean that it cannot be endorsed over to someone else; it means that if it is endorsed to someone else, that person has no more title to it than the payee. This forms some sort of protection for the drawer if the cheque is stolen and endorsed by the thief to someone else.

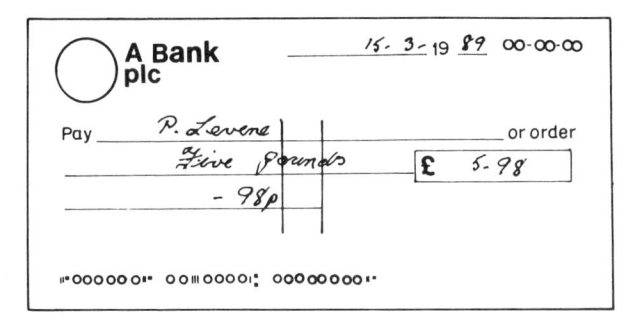

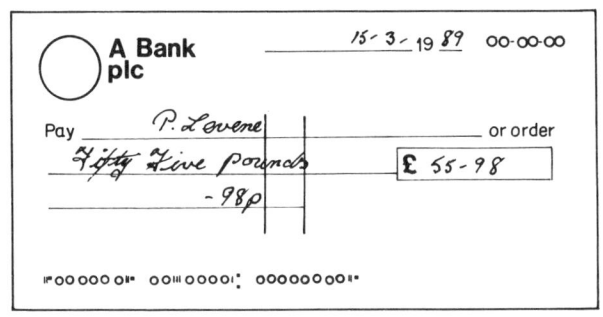

Write fewer cheques Write as few cheques as possible, perhaps by adding together two or more invoices for the same supplier.

Spare cheque books How many times have you found yourself stranded without a cheque book either because you forgot to order another in time or because of a postal or printer's dispute? Whilst having a genuine reason for not paying someone may be useful on occasions, it can also prove embarrassing or even annoying. The solution to this problem is to always keep a spare cheque book in a safe place ready for use. A spare paying-in book also comes in handy.

Bank Charges

Frequency of banking There are several ways in which bank charges can be kept down. For instance, do not pay in more credits than necessary. In deciding what is necessary, consideration has to be given to:

(a) Security problems at the shop.
(b) Clearing your customers' cheques without too much delay.

(c) The need to keep funds flowing into the bank account to meet drawn cheques, standing orders, maintain a credit balance or reduce an overdraft. In other words, do not bank twice a day every day, e.g. assuming your bank is charging you 50p per credit, you would be paying £5 per week in charges. Cut this down to twice per week and you will save £208 per year!

Small cheques—investment a/c   You can reduce your bank charges by paying small cheques into an investment account and leaving them until either you need the money or they have amounted to a sufficient figure to pay one of your bills.

Private accounts   Always have a personal account as well as a business account, and put as much as you can through the private account to save charges.

Cheque cards   Ensuring that cheques are accepted only with cheque cards should ensure that none is returned unpaid. Apart from losing the amount of the cheque you will also be charged by the bank for processing unpaid cheques and for advising you of their return. (See also page 86.)

Pay cash whenever possible   Keep the amount of cash you pay in to a minimum by paying wages, bills, etc. out of takings whenever possible, rather than having to draw separate cheques to make these payments.

Insufficient money in account   Try not to draw cheques when there is insufficient money in the account. If you do you may incur a charge to cover the cost of the bank having to write to you about an overdrawn balance; or even worse, if your cheques are returned there will be a charge for processing the unpaid cheques and returning them to the payees banks.

Credit terms   Take advantage of all credit terms allowed by your suppliers. This will benefit your account by either keeping your credit balance higher and improving the allowance on balances which is deducted from the account charge, or reducing an overdraft and thus keeping down interest charges.

Charges for interviews and letters   Some banks charge for interviews and for letters written to customers. Some also charge for providing statements if they are required more frequently than once a month.

Excessive charges—other banks   Most bank fees and charges are negotiable. If you consider your bank charges excessive, talk to your bank manager, ask him how they are costed and whether he can do it on a different basis to reduce these charges. If you are still dissatisfied talk to other banks and see what their charges would be, or use the National Girobank.

Paying Expenses Through a Building Society

If you do not have a loan or an overdraft from your bank think about transferring a fixed sum of money each week into a building society account, the type which provides you with a cheque book, so that you can earn extra interest—far more than the small amount allowed by banks on your cleared balance which is offset against their charges. It works like this: add together an actual or estimated yearly amount for rent, rates, insurance, accountancy, electricity, telephone, etc., and then divide by 52 weeks. Start the account with some surplus cash, and then transfer the required amount each week. When the bills become due, pay them with a building society cheque. Whenever there is an increase in rent, rates, etc., simply update the weekly transfer amount.

Banking (Security)

When banking cash, care should be taken to vary the route, days and the time as much as possible, and do not walk along the road carrying cash bags or paying-in books so that everyone can see.

Insurance

'Shop Package' Insurance

Look for the following in a 'package' insurance policy apart from cover of stock, shop fittings and equipment:

(1) If your keys are lost or stolen does it cover the cost of new locks?
(2) Are you reimbursed for loss of trading if you have to close because of some event beyond your control, and will your accountant's charges for certifying the claim be reimbursed also?
(3) Does loss of 'money' also include cheques and postal orders?
(4) Do you get compensation if you are injured in a robbery or hold-up in the shop?
(5) How much is the limit on the 'public liability' section? It should be approximately £1 million.
(6) Are you covered for 'wrongful arrest' if you mistakenly accuse someone of stealing from you?

Shopkeeper's Combined Policies

If you have a shopkeeper's combined policy look to see that it covers all eventualities. If it is too limited you can either add extra insurance to it, or take out a separate policy.

Material Facts

When you complete a proposal form for insurance purposes you are asked to set down any 'material facts' which might alter the risk and thus the premium requested. The question is not whether, in your opinion, a fact is 'material' or not, but whether an insurance company would consider it to be something they should know about when setting the premium. If a fact, which they decide is material emerges after a claim, they can disclaim liability and refuse to pay, regardless of how many years you have paid your premium. This is why it is always better to disclose anything that could possibly be construed 'material' by the insurance company, and certainly any events, circumstances or information of changes since the last premium, when renewing the policy.

Policies

Examine your insurance policy thoroughly, and if you have any doubts or queries deal with them immediately. It is too late once you need to make a claim.

Insuring Stock—Deliveries After Stocktaking

When placing a value on your stock for insurance purposes, do not blindly write down the amounts on your last stocktake, but consider whether or not the figures are a true reflection of your *normal* stock. For instance, did you run down or delay delivery of various items? A large delivery two days after stocktaking can make nonsense of your stock figure as far as insurance is concerned.

Averaging

Make sure you are insured for your full stock value, or you may fall prey to the law of 'averaging'. It works like this: if your stock value is £12,000 and you insure it for £6,000, the insurance company will assume you are taking half the risk yourself and will only pay half the loss, even though this amount may be a lot less than £6,000. If you feel this may apply to you make sure your stock is as low as possible when the assessor comes to inspect!

Different Types of Stock

If you alter or add to the type of goods you are selling—particularly if you start selling videos, tobacco, off licence goods, jewellery, etc.—inform your insurance company immediately, otherwise they may refuse to pay out if you are unfortunate enough to suffer a break-in.

Phone cards Likewise, if you start selling phonecards inform your insurance company and find out which category they will be insured under.

Valid Car Insurance

Did you know that almost all motor vehicle insurance policies contain a clause which says that the vehicle must be kept in a roadworthy condition for the policy to be valid? This means that if you have an accident and, for instance, the tyres were found to be bald, the insurance company would be within its rights to refuse the claim.

Conditions of Policy

Make sure you comply with any conditions laid down by your insurance company such as having window shutters or a recognised burglar alarm system installed. If you do not it could invalidate any claim you may have.

Theft

Thefts not covered   Are you as fully covered for burglary and theft as you think you are? For instance, if you catch an assistant stealing from you, the insurance company will not pay up because policies do not cover theft from within. If you leave a window open or forget to lock the front door and someone enters your shop and steals all your stock, you will not be covered because there is no forcible entry. If you have a criminal record and have not informed the insurance company, they may not pay up if they find out because they ask for any material facts to be disclosed. Material facts are anything an insurer thinks may influence acceptance or assessment of the risks proposed.

Thieves—no forceful entry   Did you know that insurance companies will not generally accept liability for losses where entry has not been gained by forcible and violent means, or the owner or staff has not been threatened? This is understandable for the thief who pinches a packet of Smarties or half a bottle of whisky, but how do you stand if someone picks up your till and runs off with it, or if they walk through your shop into your private accommodation and steal your video, television, etc., etc., and walk out through your back door? It is worth checking with your insurance company to see how you stand.

Theft of goods from car/van   Make sure you have cover for everything needed in your shop. For instance, does your policy cover you if you have goods stolen from your car or van? This is not the same as 'goods in transit'.

Claiming

Telephone your insurance company as soon after the event as possible. If the company insists on a figure before you are able to find out the full extent of the claim, sign the claim form, but qualify it by adding 'at this date'.

Loss assessors If you have a substantial loss the insurance company will appoint a loss adjustor to settle the claim. If you foresee any problems it may be wise to instruct a loss *assessor* to act for you. He will negotiate the best terms he can with the loss adjustor. His fee depends on the amount of the claim, so he has an incentive to get the best deal he can for you. Find out exactly what this fee will be before you give him the go-ahead.

Full and final settlement Once an insurance claim has been agreed you will be asked to sign and return a form stating that payment will be made in 'full and final settlement' of the claim. Check carefully that everything has been accounted for before returning this form because having done so, no further claim about this occurrence will be accepted by the insurance company.

Claim arguments If you have an argument with your insurance company and they refuse to pay, you can contact The Consumer Affairs Department, The Association of British Insurers, Aldermary House, Queen Street, London EC4N 1TU. Telephone: 01 248 4477. This is an independent body which can take up individuals' claims and in certain circumstances can order your insurance company to pay up. You can also write to The Insurance Ombudsman Bureau, 31 Southampton Row, London, WC1B 5HJ. Telephone: 01 242 8613.

Employer's Liability

If you employ staff you must have employer's liability insurance, and a copy of the insurance certificate should be displayed in the shop. You can be prosecuted if you fail to do this.

Health Insurance

If you are thinking of taking out a health insurance policy, find out the date cover actually commences. In many cases this is not for at least 30 days in order to protect the company from claims by people who know they are already ill. Enquire from several companies to see if they include this clause, or if cover commences immediately as with motor car insurance.

Brokers

If you are having problems with an insurance broker contact The British' Insurance Brokers' Association, 14 Bevis Marks, London, EC3A 7NT. Telephone: 01 623 9043.

Pensions

Your Responsibility

As you are aware, being self-employed means the buck stops with you. If you do not think about your future income when you retire, no one else will.

State Pensions

It is likely that the basic state pension, to which everyone over retirement age is entitled, will not keep anyone in clover, so, if you can manage to save something towards a private pension you should do so.

Tax Concessions

The government tries to encourage you to save this way by making two big tax concessions. First, all contributions qualify at the full rate for tax relief. Secondly, the pension funds themselves are allowed to grow free of tax, which means your nest egg will grow faster.

Payments—Monthly/Annually

An important advantage of pension plans over endowment insurance policies is that you can vary the amounts you pay from year to year according to how well or badly the business has fared during the past trading year. You can either pay monthly or you can leave it until the end of your financial year, and then pay a lump sum according to what you feel you can afford.

Account Books

Procrastination

Is there something you have to do at regular intervals, but you keep putting it off because you do not feel like it? The best way of dealing with this problem is to sit down and work out the most suitable time of day/week/month this chore has to be done, and then start doing it. Once you get into the routine it will not feel half so bad, and will be over and done with before you know it.

Filing and Bookwork

Keep your filing and bookwork in order. It will save you money as well as preventing headaches and stress at a later date. Set aside a definite time each week for this chore. Get into a routine and stick to it.

VAT Return

Another reason to keep your books in order weekly is to dispose of the VAT 'headache'. With the *Clear 'n' Easy Accounts Book* this only takes a few minutes, so complete the return as quickly as possible. After all, if you owe them money you do not have to send it until the end of the month, but if they owe you, why not get it as soon as possible?

Figures in Pencil

When completing your accounts book enter all figures in pencil until such time as the whole week's balance has been agreed, and then ink in.

Complete All Sections of Accounts Book

When using a shopkeeper's accounts book such as my *Clear 'n' Easy*, make sure you fill in all the sections. They are all important.

Bank Balance Section

Always fill in the 'bank balance' section of the accounts book, and update it if necessary when you receive a bank statement. That way you will always know how much is in the bank.

Cash Balance

The 'cash balance' should also be maintained and the 'cash carried forward' figure checked against the actual cash you have in hand. If there is a discrepancy, you have missed something out.

Alter Headings

Do not be afraid to alter headings in accounts books if necessary. For instance, in the *Clear 'n' Easy Accounts Book* there are spaces for two additional rates of VAT should they ever be introduced. One of these is ideal to record daily takings of Christmas Club receipts which have been rung up on a separate department on the till. A system like this is essential to save complete confusion with Christmas Club receipts.

Mess and stress Remember the slogan 'more mess, more stress' as far as bookwork is concerned.

Cash Payments Entered

Enter details of all cash payments for goods and expenses as soon as you can lest you forget or lose an invoice. Any amount not written down leads to an inflated profit, and a higher income tax demand.

Expenses Not Listed

Every £100 worth of expenses not listed will cost you at least approximately £25.

Paying for petrol How often do you pay cash for your petrol, then lose the receipt and forget to enter it into your accounts book? This can prove very costly over the course of a year because it means you will show an increase in your yearly net profit, and this will result in you paying more income tax than you need. It is much more sensible to pay by credit card, and also obtain the benefit of an extra month's credit.

Unusual Transactions

Make sure complete details of any unusual business are included and a written explanation is placed alongside. The more information you include in your accounts book, the easier it will be for your accountant, and in theory at least, the cheaper his bill will be.

Pets

If you own cats or dogs you can charge both their vets' bills and their food to the business. Cats are a form of rodent control, and dogs are part of the shop's security.

Enter Whole Pounds

When entering your takings into your accounts book, you will find it quicker and easier to ignore any pence and just write down the whole pounds. The odd pence shoud be rung up as the first takings of the following day.

Check Costs Regularly

Check your current expenses regularly. Only by doing this can you see how profitable or not your shop is becoming.

Graphs To keep a record of how your shop is doing throughout the year, and to get a comparison with the past few years, a graph of takings is essential. This is how to do it.

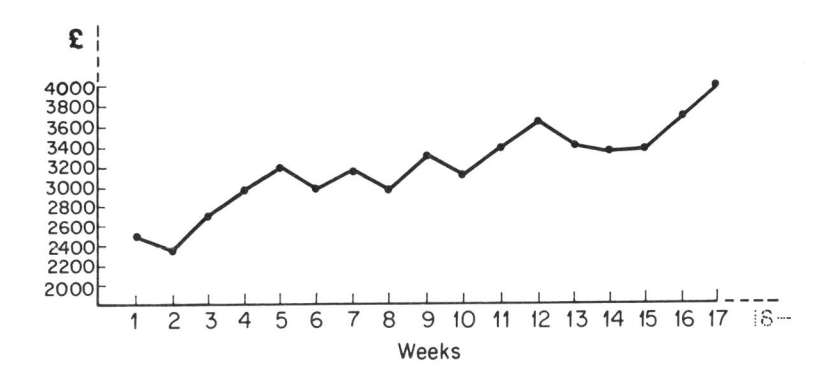

Use a sheet of graph paper wide enough to accommodate 52 weeks. Make sure the takings column is long enough to cover future inflation and general increase in trade. Draw each year in a different colour, and a break-even line at the start of each year.

Separate graphs   Graphs for other facets of the business, apart from sales, can also be very useful. If you enjoy doing this sort of thing you could make separate graphs for the following: number of customers; estimated net profit weekly; separate graphs for each day; and so on. They do take a little time, but the end results can be very rewarding.

Summary sheet   Together with the graph of weekly sales you should also keep a summary sheet showing unusual trading conditions such as 'snow', 'bus strike', 'opening of nearby superstore', 'heatwave', etc. On this sheet you could also keep a note of seasonal sales and orders, such as 'sold 195 loaves of bread, Christmas, or 'sold out 1.30p.m. Hot Cross buns—order 450 next year', etc.

How Much Are Your Total Expenses Per Week?

Do you know how much it costs you to live and survive each week? You should. To find out, take a fairly large sheet of paper and start by listing all your shop expenses down the left-hand side, and the total *yearly* cost beside each. Make all these figures as up-to-date as possible. If you do not know a figure, look back at last year's accounts and add something for inflation. You should include such items as rent, rates, water rates, shop contents insurance, building insurance, telephone, gas/electricity, advertising, bags and wrapping, till rolls and labels, postage, mortgage/loan, HP, leasing, repairs and renewals, bank charges, accountant's fees, staff wages, etc. With regard to wages, do not forget to make an allowance for extra staff to replace those on holiday, or to replace you if you take a holiday. Leave a few spaces and then list your motor car expenses: motor tax, insurance, petrol, oil, servicing and repairs, and repayments, if any. The last section is comprised of your personal expenditure. List yearly amounts spent on food, clothing, personal insurance, entertainment, HP, etc., and a figure to cover unexpected events. If you live privately in a house, you will also have to add to this section household expenses such as telephone, gas, electricity, rates, water rates, mortgage, etc. Make a subtotal beneath each section, and a grand total right at the bottom. As soon as anything is altered—for example if your wife decides she needs more money for food or you cut the hours of a member of staff, etc.—an updated figure should be entered to the right of the old one and new totals arrived at. Divide this figure by 52 and you will know how much profit you have to make each week simply to cover your costs.

Try to cut expenses   Study each item of shop expenses very carefully and try to make savings in as many sections as possible. If you can reduce this figure by even £500, that is £500 extra net profit per annum. That is enough to pay for your car tax, television licence, National Insurance stamps, and a couple of cases of whisky to calm your nerves!

What Gross Profit Are You Working On?

To find out what your gross profit is, you will need to start by listing all the firms you deal with, and then taking each in turn look back over a sufficiently long period to be able to work out first an average weekly spend with each, and secondly a gross profit percentage with each. It is not as daunting as it sounds to find an average percentage of profit for each firm because you will generally find that these figures are very similar. For example, if you study the last three accounts for Company 'X' you will probably find they give you near enough the same profit margin. Having done this, extend the figures for each company to give a cash profit and a total retail value. A simplified example is shown below.

	Wholesale		Retail	Cash Profit
Company A	1512 @ 16%	(mark-up)	1800	288
Company B	294 @ 25%		392	98
Company C	383 @ 28%		532	149
Company D	80 @ 35%		123	43
Company E	200 @ 20%		250	50
			3097	628

On the above example of takings of £3,097.00 per week, the gross profit is 20.2 per cent (628/3097 × 100).

How Much Are You Losing?

You can find out how much you have lost in the past year by comparing the gross profit on your accounts to that which you have discovered above. For instance, if you are showing 17 per cent on your accounts, you are losing approximately 3.2 per cent (20.2–17) of your turnover, or £99 per week! Some of this may be due to home consumption.

Home Consumption If your gross profit margin is not as high as you think it should be, you will have to make sure your own house is in order before knowing how much blame to place on others. Take a little time and think of each member of the family in turn. How many smoke? Is each packet of cigarettes paid for? And what about the chocolates, cakes, ice cream, etc? Although you are not stealing if you take a packet of cigarettes off the shelf without ringing it up, you should remember that this action has exactly the same effect on your gross profit margin as if the packet of cigarettes had been stolen by a customer.

Can You Afford a New Car/Fridge/Holiday, etc?

One of the things that confuses not only those new to business but also most of those who do have experience, is how to find out exactly how you are doing financially. For instance, do you know how much you earned last week after paying all expenses? If you have followed this section so far you will already know what percentage of profit you are working on and how much your weekly expenses are. It is a simple matter to relate the two. For instance, if you took £3,250.00 last week at 20.2 per cent, and your weekly expenses amount to £585, you would have had £71.50 over ([3250/100 × 20.2] − 585). A chart similar to the one below will keep you informed of the current state of your business.

Gross Profit (22%)	720	760	635	690
Normal Expenses	650	650	650	650
Extra "	—	—	—	—
Weekly +/−	70 +	110 +	15 −	40 +
Total +/−	70 +	180 +	165 +	205 +

Extra Expenditure—Project for Next Accounts

When you are thinking of an extra item of expenditure, such as another member of staff or a new car, and wonder how it will affect your profitability, work it out on the basis of the following year's trading. Take into account possible future increases in rent, rates, wages, etc., and also project a turnover figure. If you have been completing a takings graph you should be able to see trends and have a good idea on this. Assuming your gross profit margin remains the same, you will be able to produce a projected trading account and net profit for the following year, and after comparing it with your last set of accounts you will be able to see exactly how much the investment will cost you.

Calculator 'memory' Hardly anyone uses the 'memory' function on a calculator, yet it is one of the most useful and time saving features on it. For instance, if you have to total a list of numbers, it takes no longer to press the 'M +' button than it does the ordinary ' + '. The benefit is that if you are interrupted in the middle of the addition, the last amount entered will be shown on the display, whereas if you use the ' + ' sign, the total so far will be shown, which will not help at all.

Memory and bookwork Another major benefit of using the memory is found when completing the bookwork. The following simplified example based on the *Clear 'n' Easy Traders Accounts Book* will demonstrate this. Take out a calculator and follow the method.

	A Cash	B Cheque	C Zero	D Standard	E VAT
Butcher		56.29	56.29		
Baker	124.50		97.20	23.74	3.56
Candlestick Maker	23.00	100.00		106.96	16.04
	147.50	156.29	153.49	130.70	19.60

Add 'A' amounts into 'M + '. For total press 'MR'. Add 'B' amounts into ordinary ' + ', then put this figure into 'M + '. Add 'C' figures into ' + ', then put this figure into 'M − '. Total the figures for 'D' and 'E' and put them into 'M − '. Then press 'MR'. If the answer displayed is '0', all the figures are accurate. You have proved them all and do not need to check each column again.

Computer statements

08/7/88	17864	CRDT	12.00 −
11/7/88	17962	INV	909.24 +
11/7/88	18018	INV	50.77 +
11/7/88	18123	INV	81.49 +
12/7/88	18237	CRDT	2.60 −
12/7/88	18306	CRDT	5.67 −
13/7/88	18471	INV	175.18 +

Computer statements, such as the one shown above, can be checked more easily on a calculator if the memory buttons 'M − ' and 'M + ' are used instead of the normal ' + ' and ' − ' signs. If you punch in the amount followed by the appropriate memory button, you can then obtain a total at any time by pressing the memory recall (MR) button.

Accountants

The law does not require you to use a qualified accountant for your yearly returns unless you are a limited company.

When choosing an accountant, personal recommendation is best. Failing that, look through Yellow Pages for *chartered* accountants, and write to several describing your type of business and the services you require, and asking if they specialise in your type of business and if they could give you a rough estimate of the cost of the work you would like done. If you are later dissatisfied with the one you select, do not be afraid to change and tell your new accountant the reason why.

Tax

Tax Evasion and Tax Avoidance

Tax evasion is an offence, but tax avoidance is perfectly legal and should be practised at every opportunity. Tax avoidance means avoiding paying tax unnecessarily on allowable services, expenses, etc.

Keep First Year Profits Low

Sole traders and partnerships should plan to keep the first year profits as low as possible, because these accounts will form the taxable basis for early years.

Reducing Tax

Tax on a full year's profits may be avoided by sole traders and partnerships if they admit a new partner, or by a partner leaving or retiring.

Loss Relief

If a business is making a loss it can be useful to end the business after April 5 so that loss relief is available for the year in which trading ends.

Retiring and Selling

If you plan to retire or sell your business, discuss the matter with your accountant first because there are special rules and definite tax advantages for selling at certain times of the year. Generally speaking, if profits are falling, it may be better to sell the business before next April 6, but to wait until early in the next year if they are rising.

VAT

Buying a business Make sure you are not charged VAT on goods when buying a business. The vendor is the person who reclaims the VAT element on his next return. There are only two exceptions when VAT has to be paid: when the purchaser does not have a VAT number, and when the vendor has more than one business trading under the same VAT number.

Change schemes retrospectively The VAT officer usually makes a first inspection for new businesses within 18 months. Up until that time you are allowed to change schemes retrospectively.

Changing schemes under £120,000 p.a. If your sales are less than £120,000 per annum you can change schemes at any time and also include sales and purchases which have been made up to three years earlier.

VAT changes If you change your name, your address, or your style of trading, or if you cease to trade, you should notify your local VAT office within 30 days, or you may incur a civil penalty.

VAT visits If you are to have a visit by a VAT officer make sure you have all your business records to hand. These include balance sheets and profit and loss accounts, bank statements, invoices, and bookkeeping records. Failure to have everything there will only delay matters and may make the officer think you have something to hide.

Units Post office salaries are based on units. A unit is a transaction evaluated at 18 seconds of paid for time.

Advice VAT/trading standards, etc. If you run into problems or have any queries regarding government legislation, VAT, health, trading standards, etc., do not be afraid to give the relevant department a ring and ask for advice. Remember, they are there to help you.

General Bookwork

Extending Your Credit Periods

You can improve your bank balance and help your cash flow situation if you lengthen your credit terms. For instance, if you pay someone weekly, ask if you could pay fortnightly instead. If you pay fortnightly, try to extend it to three weekly. Most suppliers are more interested in receiving regular payments to time, than they are in the amount outstanding, so make a point of paying when you say you will. That way, you may be able to extend the period even further in future.

Credit and Returns Books

It is very easy to return damaged goods or ask for credit for an item on which you have been overcharged, and then forget all about it, ultimately not knowing whether you have actually received a credit note or not. The simplest and most efficient way of monitoring this is to use a book specifically for this purpose. An ordinary exercise book will do. Rule out the following columns and *do not forget to fill it in* not only when claiming, but also when the credit note arrives.

Invoice No.	Date	Item	Price	Query	Date notified	Credit	Date recv'd
A604751	18/9	Twix	6.06	P/M 16p	19/9		

Checking Invoices

Check all invoices whether from a small local supplier or from a large company on a computer print-out. Everyone is capable of making mistakes, even the people who operate computers.

Computer Print-Outs

If you receive with your delivery a computer print-out invoice showing recommended retail prices and the percentage of profit for each line if sold at those prices, the first thing you should do is to cast your eye down the percentage column looking for any unduly low percentages. These may be the result of a promotion, or they could be a mistake by the computer operator. Typical errors occur when a pack size changes but the wholesale and retail prices do not, and a box of 12 is sent out instead of a box of 24, or when a price rise occurs and the wholesale price is increased, but not the retail.

Filing

When filing invoices or delivery notes always place them at the back of a file, so that the oldest and next to pay are automatically in the front.

Storing 'Paid' Invoices and Statements

A simple and effective method of storing paid invoices is to place them all into a large envelope at the end of the week once they have been entered into your accounts book, and then write on the outside of the envelope the week number corresponding to your accounts book, and the date. For example, 'WEEK 1, Week Ending 12/4/89.'

Safe places Do you often spend ages looking for something you have put in a 'safe place'? The easiest way of deciding where to put a certain item, is to work from the other end. In other words, say to yourself 'If I were looking for a . . ., where would I look?' Having decided where you would look, all you need do is hide it there.

Money-off Coupons

Money-off coupons, as most shopkeepers will agree, are a confounded nuisance. A proportion usually get lost or go out of date, and these provide extra profit for the manufacturers. The result is that the shopkeeper usually makes a loss on each item sold where coupons are not redeemed. Get into the habit of sending these coupons off regularly each week, even if there are only one or two. Your postage is refunded, and a handling allowance is usually added. Make the manufacturer pay for his money-off coupons!

Recorded delivery It is a good idea to use the recorded delivery service when sending money-off coupons for redemption, and to keep the posting receipt in a safe place in case of queries at a later date.

Write or Telephone

When requesting information or complaining it is usually better to write than to telephone. Telephone messages can easily be forgotten, so if you do phone always ask for the name of the person you are speaking to. Always keep a copy of letters you write—preferably a photocopy.

Trade Magazines

Finding the time to read interesting articles is usually a problem for the busy shopkeeper, and it is not at all unusual for a stack of unread trade magazines etc., to reach such proportions that they are discarded en masse, as being out of date, and no longer worth reading. The answer to this is to make a point of glancing quickly through each magazine or paper as soon as it is delivered, and to tear out immediately any article that looks interesting. Dispose of the rest of the paper, and study the relevant part at your leisure. What do you do with these odd bits of information that you have now had time to study? If you think they may be of use to you sometime in the future, place them in a ring binder or cardboard folder, and index them on a separate sheet. One day when you have nothing to do, look through the index—it is odds on you will be spurred into some sort of action!

CHAPTER 10

Buying and Selling a Shop

'Every man is the architect of his own future.'

Selling

Borrow Heavily, Buy Run Down Shop, Then Sell

The biggest gains are to be made from taking the biggest risks. Borrowing heavily to purchase a run down shop with real potential, building the trade up, and then selling it, is a formula that has made many people rich. The secret is to sell it as soon as it has reached its potential, and then start again. The drawbacks are twofold:

(1) If there is a dramatic rise in interest rates you may be in trouble.
(2) If the shop does not really steam ahead you will be in trouble again.

You need a good eye for a bargain, and strong nerves to do this.

Assigning Leases

There is much confusion regarding the role of the landlord when selling a leasehold shop. If the lease states that you cannot assign it without the landlord's permission, this means that permission cannot be unreasonably withheld. It cannot be that he does not like the look of the person, for instance. It must be for a very good, definite reason such as the person cannot be trusted to pay the rent (the landlord will have to prove this) or that he will use the premises for an immoral purpose. If there is a dispute it can usually be settled fairly quickly in the county court. If the clause says that you cannot assign the lease, there is not a lot you can do. You should not have bought it in the first place!

BUYING AND SELLING A SHOP

Rent Arrears

Not many people realise that a tenant, even after he has disposed of a lease, can still be responsible to the landlord for any rent arrears or damage by his successors for the remainder of the term of the lease. This is because, generally speaking, anyone who signs a lease agrees to be bound by all the conditions of that lease for the entire length of the lease period. So, in plain English, if you, as the original tenant, transferred the lease of your shop to someone who decided not to pay any rent, the landlord could eventually come to you for the arrears. This did in fact happen fairly recently in the case of an office lease, and the original tenant had to pay £48,000 rent arrears. There are moves afoot at present to reform this law so that all obligations will generally cease once a lease is transferred.

Thieves 'Casing the Joint'

If you are thinking of selling your shop, or have it on the market at present, be very careful of people coming to view. Over the past few years there has been a sizeable increase in the number of break-ins that have occurred in these circumstances. Thieves pose as potential buyers and use the opportunity to 'case the joint' and see what is worth stealing. It is good practice to ensure that nothing of real value is displayed in the shop, the stockroom, or the home, and to talk casually about your security system and burglar alarm, even if you do not have one.

Payment of Legal Fees

When you are buying or selling a property, and you are absolutely certain you wish to proceed, but you are not too sure of the other party, it is worth suggesting a separate agreement be made to the effect that if one party pulls out, they will pay all or part of the other side's legal fees. This will give a good indication of their intentions.

Capital Gains Tax on Retirement

When you reach retirement age and dispose of your business, you may be exempt from Capital Gains Tax on gains of up to £125,000, and only be charged 50 per cent for gains between £125,000 and £500,000. You can only claim the full retirement relief after you reach the age of 60 and if for the 10 years before its disposal you had owned the business or a partnership share in it. If the period is less than 10 years, you get a proportion of the full relief at the rate of £12,500 per year, for each full year of ownership.

Buying

Return on Investment

When you buy a business you are investing your capital. You should get a return on your investment of at least 20 per cent. To find out what sort of return you are getting, follow this equation:

$$\frac{\text{net profit} \times 100}{\text{capital}} = \text{return per annum}$$

Capital is the total cost of the shop including fittings, goodwill and stock. Example: If you paid £45,000 including stock for a shop showing £10,200 net profit you would get:

$$\frac{10{,}200 \times 100}{45{,}000} = 22.66\%, \text{ which is good.}$$

Valuing a Business

You can also use this system to value a business using the following equation:

$$\frac{\text{net profit} \times 100}{\text{return}} = \text{Value}$$

For instance, if the net profit is £9,350 and you are looking for a return on your investment of 20 per cent, the equation is

$$\frac{9350 \times 100}{20} = £46{,}750$$

including stock.

If you are looking for a 25 per cent return, then

$$\frac{9350 \times 100}{25} = £37{,}400.$$

Why is the Shop on the Market?

Most shops are sold for a reason. That reason is usually trade or profit has started to slip, or is about to. Your job when viewing a business is first to see if you can make an adequate living there and, if so, to try to find out why the shop is on the market. Check on the following areas:

(1) Has another shop started trading in your goods and has drawn some of the custom?
(2) Has a key shop on the parade closed, e.g. a post office, and the public are now using another parade?
(3) Has a local factory or office block moved/closed down, or is about to?
(4) Is it a dying type of trade?
(5) Is the country in a recession and all trades are suffering?
(6) Has a new bus route been introduced/cut out/re-routed?
(7) Have yellow lines been painted outside, or are they likely to be?
(8) Has the owner just lost interest?
(9) Is the shop understocked?
(10) Has a rent review just occurred, or is one about to?

Having satisfied yourself as much as possible on the above, now ask yourself the following questions:

(1) How much money do I need to spend on the shop front/floor/equipment/fixtures and fittings/general repairs?
(2) Is the range of goods sufficient?
(3) Could any lines be added?
(4) Is the stock well displayed?
(5) Does staff attitude encourage customers to return?
(6) Can the shop be extended by knocking down a wall or by extending to the side or back?
(7) Could you live in the accommodation?
(8) What are the other shops on the parade like? How does it compare to other parades?
(9) Is there anywhere for customers to park?
(10) Do you think customers will carry on using the parade?
and final question:
(11) Could the trade be improved by smartening up the shop, extending the sales area, enlarging the stock, or changing the attitudes of the present staff? If so, how much would it cost, and would it be worth it?

Find Out About Future Plans for the Area

Find out as much as possible about the surrounding area. Have a talk with the planning officer to see if there are any concrete or tentative future plans for motorways, housing developments or commercial ventures. The more you can find out about the area before you exchange contracts the safer you will be.

Local Bank Managers

If you are seriously thinking about buying a particular shop, a visit to the manager of the local bank can be very revealing, especially if you ask for a hefty loan to help with the purchase. It does not matter whether you need the loan or not. With a bit of luck the vendor will have his bank account there, and although the manager will not discuss the shop's finances, his willingness or not to offer the loan will be a great pointer to the shop's profitability. Looking at it the worst way, even if the vendor does not bank there, the manager should have a good local knowledge of most of the businesses and future developments in the area.

Freehold or Leasehold?

Should you look for a freehold or a leasehold shop? Obviously everyone would like to own their own freehold, but pound for pound you will get a much better income from a leasehold shop than a freehold. One way of progressing to this goal is to buy as large a leasehold business as you can with as large a loan as you can. Stay there for about three years, when a substantial amount of your loan will have been repaid, and then look for an even larger shop, again taking a large loan. Carry on in this manner until either the freehold of your own shop becomes available, or until you have accumulated sufficient capital to buy the freehold shop of your choice.

Landlords

When enquiring about a leasehold shop always find out who owns the freehold. Generally speaking, local authorities are much fairer about rent increases than property companies, and private landlords fall somewhere in between. Sometimes it is very hard to contact a private landlord if you have a query, but if you hope to purchase the freehold at some stage, they could be the best option.

Copy of Lease

If you own a leasehold business you are obviously aware that you will be governed in certain respects by various clauses contained in the lease. Yet, apart from a week or so before the purchase, especially if the lease is being held as security, most people never see the document again until they sell their business. It is therefore a good idea to ask your solicitor to provide you with a photocopy of the lease, or to have a photocopy made yourself when it is sent to you for witnessing and signing. You may never need to look at it again, but if you do, you will not have any delays.

Surveys

It is always worthwhile having a survey done on a shop whether it is freehold or leasehold. If leasehold it will show exactly what the condition of the property was like when you took it over (you do not have to leave the premises in a better state of repair when you sell than when you bought it, unless it expressly states this in the contract), and the cost of the survey should be easily recovered from the vendor when you present him with a large list of repairs that need to be done.

Restrictive Covenants

When buying a shop you should always include in the contract a 'restrictive covenant' preventing the seller of the business setting up in the same trade, within a certain distance, for a set period of time. If, after signing this contract, the person breaks its terms, you can get an injunction from the court to stop him, and also obtain compensation for any losses suffered.

Breaking agreements If a person disregards an injunction they will be held in 'contempt of court', the penalties for which can be very severe, including imprisonment.

Alternative to Restrictive Covenants

If for some reason the vendor is unable or unwilling to enter into a 'restrictive covenant' clause, and you still wish to continue with the purchase, you would be well-advised to insist that he agrees to the following, as an absolute minimum:

(1) He will not trade under the name of the shop anywhere else for at least three years.
(2) He will not employ, directly or indirectly, any member of staff, past or present, for at least three years.
(3) He will not enter into direct competition with you for at least three years.

New Shop—Existing Staff

If the shop you are buying has staff who wish to stay, it is a good idea to find out in advance their names, the hours they work, and their duties, and then go in as a customer, or ask a friend to go in for you, so that you can see exactly what type of workers they are, and also what their personalities are like.

Back-dated Wages Claims

If you are taking on existing staff when buying a business, make sure you give them a new contract of employment. It makes no difference whether they are full-time or part-time. If you do not, you could find yourself liable to back-dated wages claims from before you took over, even though the previous owners were at fault.

New Customers

Be wary of a customer who says he never used your shop when the previous people had it. He will usually tell a horrendous story of how he was insulted/ignored/overcharged, etc., etc. Take most of it with a pinch of salt. No shopkeeper deliberately tries to cut his own throat by intentionally disposing of his customers. If truth were told you would probably discover that your newly found friend either deliberately kept away from the shop because he owed the proprietor money, or he was so obnoxious the owner had to get rid of him in order to keep his own sanity.

CHAPTER 11

The Law and the Shopkeeper

'It's never too late to learn.'

The Shopkeeper

Wills

If you have not made a will, read the following imaginary case history carefully and make sure something like this does not happen to you.

'Mr and Mrs Dyer bought their shop 23 years ago. The business grew, and the couple later bought a house. Mr Dyer did not believe in buying property jointly with his wife, and consequently both the house and the shop were in his name only. Even his business bank account was solely in his name. On his death the shop was valued at £150,000 and the house at £285,000—a total of £435,000. Mr Dyer had never 'got round to making a will', and died intestate. The first thing that happened was that the business bank account was 'frozen', and Mrs Dyer had great problems continuing to run the shop. However, this did not last too long, because to comply with the intestacy laws she had to sell both the shop and the house in order to pay her children £180,000 and to place £180,000 into a trust. She was allowed to keep all the personal belongings, would receive a life interest from the trust, and had the grand sum of £75,000 to buy another house.'

Everyone should make a will, especially those in business. There is enough grief and distress caused by the death of a husband or wife without having to have any additional worries about finance and running the shop. You do not have to use a solicitor for this, although if your affairs are in the least complicated, it is adviseable. Solicitors do not charge a fortune. If you decide to make out your own will, you must have it witnessed by two witnesses who are not beneficiaries and who are not married to beneficiaries. If there is no will, or the will that is left is not in order, you are said to have died intestate, and in such circumstances there are specific rules governing the division of your estate.

Even if a husband and wife buy a leasehold shop jointly, there may still be problems with the goodwill portion if one partner dies without leaving a will, although the lease will pass to the widow/er.

If the bank account is in one name only, there could be problems if that partner dies. The account will probably be frozen until probate is granted and this will obviously make the running of the shop extremely difficult. Unless there is some pressing reason against it, always arrange for either partner to be signatories.

When an unrelated partner dies the interest passes to the spouse, who may know nothing about the business, and may want an immediate equal say in the day to day running of it. In these circumstances there should always be some form of cross insurance so that if one partner dies the other has sufficient money to buy out the deceased's spouse's interest, if desired.

Leases

Revisions Although most leases will stipulate that the rent will not be reduced at revision dates, this does not mean that it will increase automatically. Never accept an increase without trying to reduce the figure yourself or through the services of a professional valuer who has knowledge of business rents in your area. He can negotiate with the landlord on your behalf if required, and will also take the case to arbitration if necessary. There is almost always a clause in the lease dealing with the procedure to be adopted if agreement cannot be reached on a new rental figure. This usually takes the form of arbitration.

When a lease ends Subject to certain conditions, the tenant must be offered a new lease on similar terms to the old one, when the current lease comes to an end. The duration of the new lease must be reasonable compared with the original, and the rent will be at the current market value. The exceptions when a landlord need not grant a new lease are:
(a) if there has been a serious breach of the repair covenant. The operative word here is 'serious'. A list of minor repairs not completed, or a particular year when the outside should have been painted and was not, would not constitute a serious breach;
(b) persistent long delays in paying the rent;
(c) any other serious breach of a covenant, however, it must be really serious, such as using the premises for illegal purposes;
(d) if the landlord is able to offer alternative comparable premises in the area on similar terms;

This is what would happen to your estate if you died, not having made a will, after any Income Tax, Inheritance Tax, and Capital Gains Tax had been paid out of it:

```
                    ┌─────────────────────────┐
                    │ If you died now, would  │
                    │ you leave a widow/er?   │
                    └─────────────────────────┘
                       YES              NO
```

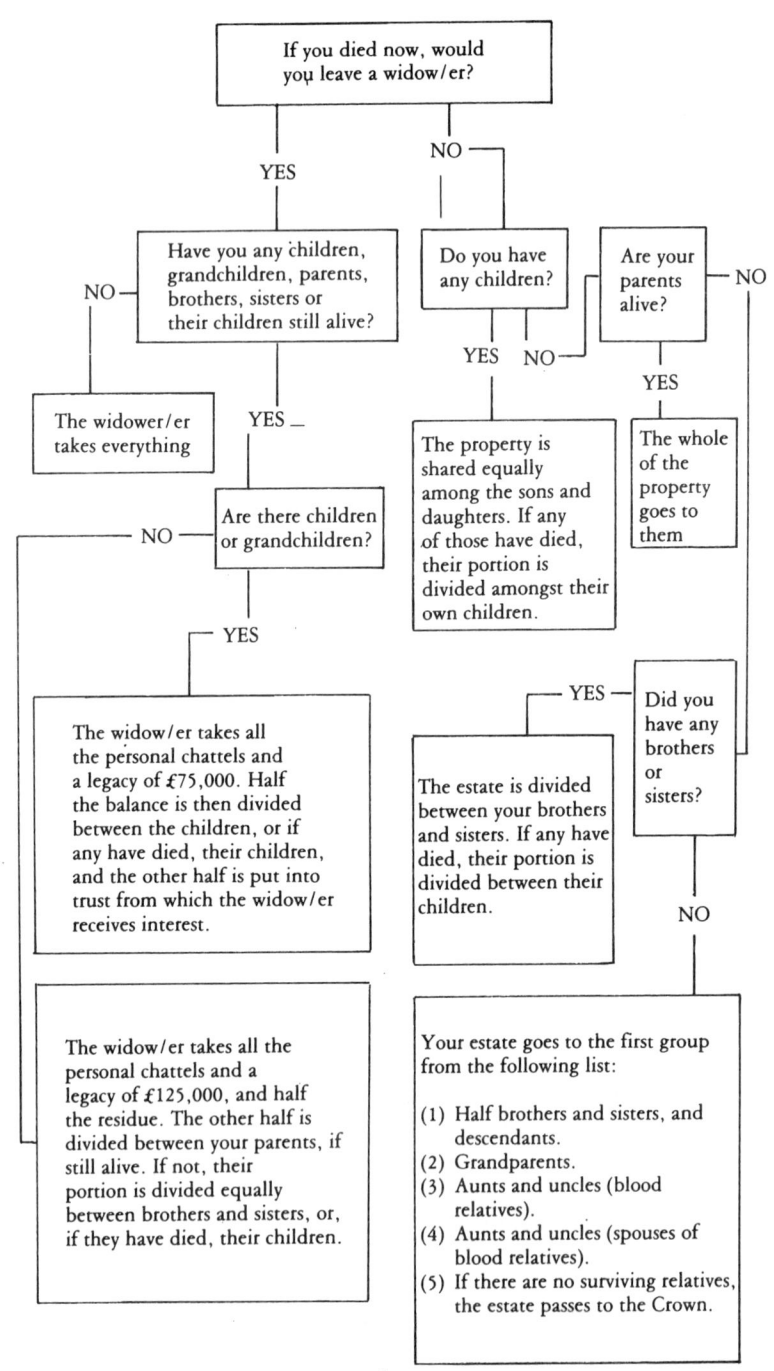

[Flowchart]

- **If you died now, would you leave a widow/er?**
  - **YES** → Have you any children, grandchildren, parents, brothers, sisters or their children still alive?
    - **NO** → The widow/er takes everything.
    - **YES** → Are there children or grandchildren?
      - **YES** → The widow/er takes all the personal chattels and a legacy of £75,000. Half the balance is then divided between the children, or if any have died, their children, and the other half is put into trust from which the widow/er receives interest.
      - **NO** → The widow/er takes all the personal chattels and a legacy of £125,000, and half the residue. The other half is divided between your parents, if still alive. If not, their portion is divided equally between brothers and sisters, or, if they have died, their children.
  - **NO** →
    - **Do you have any children?**
      - **YES** → The property is shared equally among the sons and daughters. If any of those have died, their portion is divided amongst their own children.
      - **NO** → **Are your parents alive?**
        - **YES** → The whole of the property goes to them.
        - **NO** → **Did you have any brothers or sisters?**
          - **YES** → The estate is divided between your brothers and sisters. If any have died, their portion is divided between their children.
          - **NO** → Your estate goes to the first group from the following list:
            1. Half brothers and sisters, and descendants.
            2. Grandparents.
            3. Aunts and uncles (blood relatives).
            4. Aunts and uncles (spouses of blood relatives).
            5. If there are no surviving relatives, the estate passes to the Crown.

If you do not want your estate divided as set out above make a proper will.

(e) if the lessee is occupying only part of the premises, with the rest being vacant, it may be possible to allow the landlord to be able to offer the premises as a whole;
(f) if the landlord wishes to demolish the premises for re-development and actually does;
(g) if the landlord wishes to occupy the premises for his own use, and actually does, as long as he has held an interest in the property for at least five years.

The landlord must give six months' notice and state whether or not he is prepared to offer a new lease.

If you have reason not to believe a landlord if he states that he wishes to repossess the property in order to occupy it or re-develop it, you are entitled to apply to the county court for a judgment, and unless the landlord can prove his intentions, the court is bound to order an extension to the lease.

Jury Service

If you are called for jury service at an awkward time in the shop, you can often obtain a deferral to a time which is more convenient, by contacting the summonsing office as soon as possible. The only way you can avoid jury service is if you are in one of the exempted categories, e.g. over 65, physically unable to attend, serving as a magistrate, etc.

Trial deferment   If a trial is likely to last for more than a week or two, the self-employed are generally excused for that particular trial if a request for such is made.

Compensation   You will receive compensation for the time you are away from your business.

Staff   It is an offence to impede a member of staff from performing jury service or to penalise him in any way.

Personnel

A fuller description of the following Acts may be found in *How to Start and Run Your Own Shop* (Levene, P., 1988, *How to Start and Run Your Own Shop*, Graham and Trotman, London, pages 149 to 174). Complete and up-to-date information may be obtained through contacting the relevant authority.

Sex Discrimination Act 1975

Under this Act it is unlawful for employers to discriminate on grounds of sex or against married persons. Following the Sex Discrimination Act 1986, firms with less than six employees are no longer exempt. This exception in the 1975 Act has been repealed.

Retirement—men and women It is illegal for women to be treated differently to men for most things now, including retirement. You cannot have, for example, a policy that women must retire at 60 and men at 65. It has to be the same for both.

Race Relations Act

This Act outlaws discrimination by employers on racial grounds, that is on the grounds of race, colour, nationality, or ethnic or national origins, no matter how few employees there are.

Equal Pay Acts

Employers must treat men and women alike in terms and conditions of employment where they are engaged in 'like' work. However, a difference may be made on account of seniority or extra qualifications.

Over 13 Year Olds

It is illegal to employ anyone under the age of 13, and there are many restrictions as to the hours and conditions that can be worked by over 13 year olds. The rules vary in different parts of the country and it is as well to contact your local authority to see if there are any special by-laws in your area if you are contemplating employing a youngster part-time.

Employment Bill 1989

At the time of going to print, details of a new Employment Bill were published. The main aims of this Bill are to remove outdated regulations concerning the employment of young people and to eradicate sex discrimination against women. The chief proposals are:

(1) There will be no restrictions on the hours of work for under 18 year olds. (There will be no change in the legislation for children under school leaving age, and under 18 year olds will still not be allowed to work in pubs or betting shops, or to work with dangerous machinery.)
(2) Women will now be allowed to work underground in mining and to use various types of factory machinery. The only restrictions to be kept are those where exposure to radiation or lead might harm an unborn baby.
(3) Redundancy payments for women will be granted up to the age of 65 instead of 60.
(4) Deposits of up to £150 may be requested from applicants to an industrial tribunal if the chairman considers the case has no reasonable chance of success.
(5) The period of employment needed for a worker's right to a statement of reasons for dismissal, to be extended from six months to two years.

Statutory Sick Pay (SSP)

Employers are responsible for paying SSP to all employees who are sick for four or more days in a row, apart from the following:

(a) Employees who are over state pension age on the first day of sickness.
(b) Employees who have been taken on for a specified period of no more than three months.
(c) Employees who have average weekly earnings less than the lower weekly earnings limit for national insurance contribution liability.
(d) An employee who has done no work for you under the contract of service.
(e) An expectant mother who is off sick during the time starting 11 weeks before her expected week of confinement and ending six weeks after.
(f) An employee who has already been due 28 weeks SSP from his previous employer.
(g) An employee who has a gap of 56 days or less between the end of a state benefit claim and the start of a period of incapacity for work (PIW).
(h) An employee who is in legal custody.

Statutory Maternity Pay (SMP)

Employers have to pay SMP to pregnant employees who satisfy the following conditions:

(a) She must have been continuously employed by you for at least 26 weeks continuing into the 15th week before her baby is due.
(b) She must have average weekly earnings of not less than the lower earnings limit for the payment of national insurance contributions.
(c) She must still be pregnant at the 11th week before her expected week of confinement, or have been confined by that time.
(d) She must have stopped working for you.
(e) She must have notified you at least 21 days before her absence from work is due to begin, unless you decide to accept a shorter time.
(f) She will have to produce, within an acceptable period, medical evidence showing the date the baby is due on.

Contracts

It is a legal requirement to give a written statement of terms and conditions of employment to every employee, whether full-time or part-time. You have up to 13 weeks to do this from the time employment commences. The written statement should cover such things as job title, details of wages (how much, when paid, and in what manner), holidays, holiday pay, rules about sickness and sick pay, pension arrangements, if you have any, grievance or disciplinary procedure, and the period of notice required from either side.

Itemised pay statements You should also give a written itemised pay statement showing the date, gross wage, details of any deductions made, and the amount of take home pay left.

Notice

There are set rules determining the length of notice of termination of employment required from either side, depending on the length of time the employee has worked for you.

Up to one month there are no rules. You can dismiss an employee as and when you wish. The employee can also leave you without a word of warning.

After a month there are set periods of notice depending on the length of time the employee has been employed. Up to two years is one week's notice. Over two years is one week for each completed year up to a maximum of 12 weeks, regardless of the length of employment.

Unless it is stated otherwise in the contract, employees need only give one week's notice after the first month of employment, no matter how long they have been employed.

If you do not want the employee to work the period of notice, you may send him home immediately so long as you pay for the term of notice. This is known as 'payment in lieu of notice'. Usually this is best, because someone working in these conditions is usually more of a liability than a help.

If you are dismissing someone for gross misconduct, you can do so on the spot, without giving notice.

Redundancy

Redundancy payments apply only to employees who have worked for you for more than two years.

Redundancy Pay

Employees who have not completed two years continuous employment, generally with the same employer, or who have reached age 65 for men or 60 for women, have no entitlement to redundancy pay (But see terms under proposed Employment Bill, page 130). Service under the age of 18 does not count. If you employ nine or fewer employees you can claim back 35 per cent of the payment from the Redundancy Fund. The ready reckoner for redundancy payments shown below may be taken as being accurate in most cases. Example: Man aged 54 who has worked for 8 years is entitled to 12 weeks pay. This is in addition to any notice pay.

Length of Service

Age	2	3	4	5	6	7	8	9	10	11	12	13	14	15	16	17	18	19	20
20		1	1	1	–														
21	1	1½	1½	1½	1½	–													
22	1	1½	2	2	2	2	–												
23	1	2	2½	3	3	3	3	–											
24	1½	2½	3	3½	4	4	4	4	–										
25	2	3	3½	4	4½	5	5	5	5	–									
26	2	3	4	4½	5	5½	6	6	6	6	–								
27	2	3	4	5	5½	6	6½	7	7	7	7	–							
28	2	3	4	5	6	6½	7	7½	8	8	8	8	–						
29	2	3	4	5	6	7	7½	8	8½	9	9	9	9	–					
30	2	3	4	5	6	7	8	8½	9	9½	10	10	10	10	–				
31	2	3	4	5	6	7	8	9	9½	10	10½	11	11	11	11	–			
32	2	3	4	5	6	7	8	9	10	10½	11	11½	12	12	12	12	–		
33	2	3	4	5	6	7	8	9	10	11	11½	12	12½	13	13	13	13	–	
34	2	3	4	5	6	7	8	9	10	11	12	12½	13	13½	14	14	14	14	–
35	2	3	4	5	6	7	8	9	10	11	12	13	13½	14	14½	15	15	15	15
36	2	3	4	5	6	7	8	9	10	11	12	13	14	14½	15	15½	16	16	16
37	2	3	4	5	6	7	8	9	10	11	12	13	14	15	15½	16	16½	17	17
38	2	3	4	5	6	7	8	9	10	11	12	13	14	15	16	16½	17	17½	18
39	2	3	4	5	6	7	8	9	10	11	12	13	14	15	16	17	17½	18	18½
40	2	3	4	5	6	7	8	9	10	11	12	13	14	15	16	17	18	18½	19
41	2	3	4	5	6	7	8	9	10	11	12	13	14	15	16	17	18	19	19½
42	2	3½	4½	5½	6½	7½	8½	9½	10½	11½	12½	13½	14½	15½	16½	17½	18½	19½	20½
43	2	4	5	6	7	8	9	10	11	12	13	14	15	16	17	18	19	20	21
44	2½	4½	5½	6½	7½	8½	9½	10½	11½	12½	13½	14½	15½	16½	17½	18½	19½	20½	21½
45	3	4½	6	7	8	9	10	11	12	13	14	15	16	17	18	19	20	21	22
46	3	4½	6	7½	8½	9½	10½	11½	12½	13½	14½	15½	16½	17½	18½	19½	20½	21½	22½
47	3	4½	6	7½	9	10	11	12	13	14	15	16	17	18	19	20	21	22	23
48	3	4½	6	7½	9	10½	11½	12½	13½	14½	15½	16½	17½	18½	19½	20½	21½	22½	23½
49	3	4½	6	7½	9	10½	12	13	14	15	16	17	18	19	20	21	22	23	24
50	3	4½	6	7½	9	10½	12	13½	14½	15½	16½	17½	18½	19½	20½	21½	22½	23½	24½
51	3	4½	6	7½	9	10½	12	13½	15	16	17	18	19	20	21	22	23	24	25
52	3	4½	6	7½	9	10½	12	13½	15	16½	17½	18½	19½	20½	21½	22½	23½	24½	25½
53	3	4½	6	7½	9	10½	12	13½	15	16½	18	19	20	21	22	23	24	25	26
54	3	4½	6	7½	9	10½	12	13½	15	16½	18	19½	20½	21½	22½	23½	24½	25½	26½
55	3	4½	6	7½	9	10½	12	13½	15	16½	18	19½	21	22	23	24	25	26	27
56	3	4½	6	7½	9	10½	12	13½	15	16½	18	19½	21	22½	23½	24½	25½	26½	27½
57	3	4½	6	7½	9	10½	12	13½	15	16½	18	19½	21	22½	24	25	26	27	28
58	3	4½	6	7½	9	10½	12	13½	15	16½	18	19½	21	22½	24	25½	26½	27½	28½
59	3	4½	6	7½	9	10½	12	13½	15	16½	18	19½	21	22½	24	25½	27	28	29
60	3	4½	6	7½	9	10½	12	13½	15	16½	18	19½	21	22½	24	25½	27	28½	29½
61	3	4½	6	7½	9	10½	12	13½	15	16½	18	19½	21	22½	24	25½	27	28½	30
62	3	4½	6	7½	9	10½	12	13½	15	16½	18	19½	21	22½	24	25½	27	28½	30
63	3	4½	6	7½	9	10½	12	13½	15	16½	18	19½	21	22½	24	25½	27	28½	30
64	3	4½	6	7½	9	10½	12	13½	15	16½	18	19½	21	22½	24	25½	27	28½	30

The Two Year Rule

Remember that as far as employment legislation is concerned, employees have virtually no rights at all for the first two years. So, if you are thinking of changing a member of staff, try to do so before this two year period has elapsed. You then need have no fears of unfair dismissal or possible redundancy payments. The only exception is unfair dismissal under the Sex Discrimination Act which can be instigated at anytime.

Written Statement of Dismissal

After six months employment, the employee is legally entitled to have a written statement of the reasons for dismissal, but if you are not asked for this you do not have to provide one (But see terms under the proposed Employment Bill, page 130). If you are asked, you have 14 days in which to provide it. If you do not comply, the employee can complain to an industrial tribunal.

Unfair Dismissal

'Unfair dismissal' only applies to employees who have worked for you for over two years. They then have the right to go to a tribunal if they think they have been sacked for no good reason. They must do this within three months of the date of their dismissal. You would then have to show the tribunal that you acted reasonably, and that the main cause of dismissal was one of the following:

(a) A reason related to the employee's conduct.
(b) A reason related to the employee's capability or qualification for the job.
(c) Redundancy.
(d) A statutory duty or restriction on either the employer or the employee which prevents the employment being continued.
(e) Some other 'substantial reason' which could justify the dismissal.

It is generally accepted that an employer has 'acted reasonably' towards a member of staff if he has followed the following dismissal procedure:

(1) A verbal warning is given that if no improvement is made dismissal will have to be considered.
(2) If there is no improvement a written warning is given.
(3) If there is still no improvement, and no adequate explanation offered by the employee, then a notice of dismissal is given.

You should keep a record of the dates of each of these warnings, and make the employee sign a copy of receipt of the written warning.

Reasonableness   In matters of law the word 'reasonable' keeps appearing. 'Did he take reasonable care in the circumstances?' 'Did he take reasonable precautions?' 'Would a person of reasonable intelligence have acted like that in those conditions?' and so on. Remember the word 'reasonable' when there is any query with regard to the law.

Criminal Records

It has been held that, apart from minor errors, if an employee has given false information on a job application form on matters which might have influenced the decision of the employer as to whether or not to offer the job, he can be justifiably dismissed. The one exception is the disclosure of a criminal record when the sentence was under two and a half years. After an appropriate length of time, depending on the sentence, the conviction becomes 'spent'. The individual is then protected by laws and need not admit to having been found guilty of a crime. Examples of time limits after which convictions need not be revealed and slates are wiped clean are:

(a) Sentences of six months or less become 'spent' after a period of seven years.
(b) Fines or community service become 'spent' after five years.
(c) Probation becomes 'spent' after one year.

8 to 15 Hours per Week

All of the above applies to assistants working for 16 hours or more a week. Some also apply to those working between 8 to 15 hours a week, in which case the length of employment is extended from two to five years.

Under eight hours per week   Employees working less than eight hours per week have virtually no rights at all.

Industrial Tribunals

Industrial tribunals are bodies that have been set up to deal with the multitude of employment legislation that has occurred since 1962, such as Equal Pay, Written Contracts, Maternity Pay, Racial Discrimination, Redundancy, Sex Discrimination, Unfair Dismissal, etc., etc. They are held all over the country, and are much less formal than a normal court hearing, but the verdicts they arrive at are just as binding. Each tribunal consists of three members: a chairman who is legally qualified, and two others who do not have to have any legal qualifications, but who must have a detailed knowledge of employment affairs. One represents the employers' points of view, and the other, the trade unions'. It is not necessary to be represented by a lawyer. In almost all cases each party will have to pay his own costs regardless of the outcome, unless the tribunal thinks the complaint has been made up or is frivolous. If you do not wish to attend the hearing, you need not do so. You may present your case in writing, in which case, of course, you will not be able to cross examine the other party. Broadly speaking, the normal procedure is as follows: each side has to make a written statement of the facts and a date will be set for the hearing. But before this date an officer from ACAS (Advisory Conciliation and Arbitration Service) will probably contact each side to see if things can be sorted out amicably. If not, all the evidence will be examined at the hearing and witnesses may be called to appear on your behalf. The tribunal will usually make its decision at the end of the hearing, and if it awards compensation to one party, this must be paid within 42 days or county court proceedings may be taken. Appeals against a decision can be made to the Employment Appeal Tribunal, but these must also be made within 42 days.

Solicitors—Fixed Fee Interviews

Before taking legal action it is adviseable to have a fixed fee interview with a solicitor. The Citizens Advice Bureau will have a list of solicitors in your area who provide such a service.

The Law

If you have any query regarding the law as it applies to you, the shopkeeper, contact your local Trading Standards Officer (used to be called Weights and Measures). He will be only too pleased to help. He is not there just to receive complaints from customers.

Offices, Shops and Railway Premises Act 1963

This Act applies to all shops where people are employed. It covers minimum temperatures, washing and eating facilities, lighting, etc., etc. There are also regulations stipulating the number of sanitary conveniences according to the number of employees. These state that one closet is sufficient if the number of people regularly employed at one time does not exceed five, or if each regular employee normally works in the premises for two hours daily or less. In all other cases separate sanitary accommodation must be provided for men and women, and each must be marked accordingly. The Regulations state the number of closets that have to be provided in proportion to the number of employees. The cleaning of machinery is also covered. No person under the age of 18 may clean any machinery if this exposes him to risk of injury.

A first aid box must be kept on the premises in a readily accessible position.

Heating In Shops

There is no minimum heating requirement for shops that are open to the public, although in cold weather provision should be made for staff to warm themselves from time to time.

The Customer

Photographs

You are entitled to display inside your shop or in your shop window, any photographs you take of anyone. You do not need the person's permission, even if you use him for advertising purposes, and he is not entitled to any form of privacy. It is no different to publishing photographs in newspapers or magazines.

Accidents in the Shop

Shopkeepers must take all reasonable steps to prevent accidents happening to customers in their shops. If they do not, the customer could sue for damages and be awarded compensation. Taking reasonable steps means, for instance, if something is smashed on the floor, it is cleared up immediately. So, if a customer turned into an aisle of the shop and knocked a bottle of liquid on to the floor and the woman walking immediately behind slipped and injured herself the shopkeeper would not be to blame. But if the liquid had been left on the floor for some considerable time, it would be a different story. The shopkeeper would probably be adjudged to have acted in a negligent manner. Apart from breakages on the floor, any area of the shop which could prove dangerous should be roped off, or the hazard clearly pointed out and a warning notice displayed. The hazard could be a step inside the shop, a low beam, an area by a door which is frequently opened, etc., etc. As long as you have a warning notice in a suitable position you have fulfilled your obligations and it is up to the customer to look out for himself.

Breakages If a customer knocks something over or drops it in the shop, he is legally responsible for paying for it unless it was not his fault, for instance, if it was caused through touching an unstable display. If a child accompanied by a parent damages something, the parent is responsible, but not if the child is in the shop by himself.

Pricing Goods

Misleading the public Although you do not have to sell any item for any particular price, it is an offence to try to deliberately mislead the public by having, say, one price advertised in the shop window, and a higher price inside the shop.

Displaying prices of goods By law, the only goods that have to be priced on the shelf are foods for human consumption. If these are not priced individually, a single ticket in an adjacent conspicuous position will suffice. In the case of foods which are not in a self-service display, such as those in a refrigerated serve-over counter, the only foods which have to be priced with a unit price are meat, vegetables and cheese.

Free offers If you are making a 'free offer' you must make it absolutely clear to customers what they will have to buy to get the 'free offer', and you must not inflate these prices, or make additional charges, or offer to reduce the price of these articles if the 'free offer' is not taken up.

Pricing tickets Under Part III of the Consumer Protection Act 1987 it is an offence to give a misleading price indication to your customers. This means that when you write out price tickets, you are not allowed to write whatever you wish. You must not mislead the customer, nor leave him in any doubt whatsoever as to exactly what is being offered. A few examples of ticketing follow:

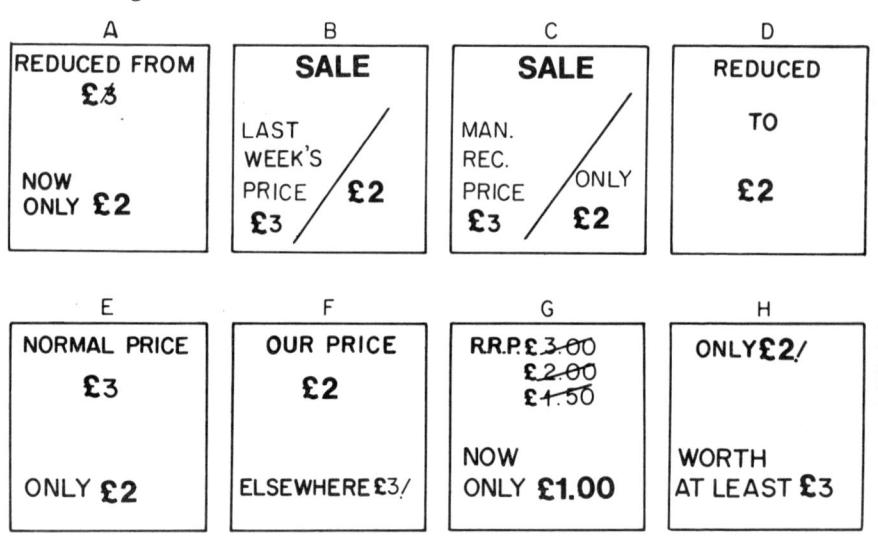

A	B	C	D
REDUCED FROM £3 NOW ONLY £2	SALE LAST WEEK'S PRICE £3 / £2	SALE MAN. REC. PRICE £3 / ONLY £2	REDUCED TO £2

E	F	G	H
NORMAL PRICE £3 ONLY £2	OUR PRICE £2 ELSEWHERE £3/	R.R.P. £3.00 £2.00 £1.50 NOW ONLY £1.00	ONLY £2/ WORTH AT LEAST £3

- 'A' £3 must be the last price the product was available to customers and you must have had that product on sale for 28 consecutive days during the last six months, unless there is a clear and precise disclaimer. This 28 day rule does not apply to food, drink or perishable goods. The article must have been on sale in your premises, not in one of a chain of your shops.
- 'B' Do not think that you need only have had the article for sale at £3 on one day during the previous week—the 28 day rule still applies.
- 'C' If you use the terms 'RRP' (recommended retail price) or 'Man. Rec. Price' (manufacturer's recommended price) you have to be sure that these prices have actually been recommended by the manufacturer or supplier.

'D' You may not use a ticket, or even suggest to the customer that the goods have been cut in price to '£x', without giving the higher price.

'E' If you use phrases such as 'regular price', 'normal price', 'usual price', etc., you have to say whose regular, normal, or usual price it is.

'F' If you want to compare prices with those of a competitor, you have to state his name and address clearly, 'elsewhere' will not be sufficient.

'G' If you reduce a price and then wish to reduce it further during the same sale, the intervening prices need not have applied for 28 days, but the highest price must have followed this rule. All the intervening prices must be shown.

'H' You must not use such words as 'worth' or 'value' for comparison when pricing an article.

Pricing—more than one ticket It is not against the law to have more than one price ticket on an article, so long as they are all visible to the customer, and you charge the lowest price shown. What is against the law is to have a higher priced ticket in a place where the customer would not expect to look, such as underneath or inside the article, and then to charge that price.

Pricing goods upwards It is not illegal to price goods upwards, which are already on the shop shelves at a certain price. This includes food. If you do this, always remove the old tickets.

Price increases of goods ordered If a customer asks you to order something, and it comes in at a higher price, the customer may say that it was only '£x' when ordered, and that is all he will pay. In this case you may have a problem. It depends on whether you actually discussed the price at the time of the order. If you both agreed the price was '£x' then the likelihood is that that is what must be paid. If the price was not mentioned, then it is reasonable to assume with inflation that the price will be higher, depending, of course, on the length of time the order takes to come through. To avoid any misunderstandings at a later date it is always best to make it clear that the price will be that which is ruling at the time of delivery.

Contracts—sale of goods If you inadvertently put the wrong price on an article, you do not have to accept that price, regardless what anyone says. For example, if you were not concentrating and priced an item at 25p instead of £25, no one would have any 'rights' to buy that item for 25p. In fact, even if you priced the item correctly, no one would have any 'rights' to buy it, anyway. Every sale involves making a verbal contract, and each simple contract has three elements: an *offer*, an *acceptance*, and a *consideration*. When an article is priced, it is an 'invitation to treat', or in other words, an invitation to the customer to make an *offer*. It is up to the shopkeeper to decide whether or not to *accept* the offer. If he does, he hands the goods to the customer, who provides the *consideration* by paying.

Legal tender Bank of England notes and coins are legal tender throughout the United Kingdom. Scottish and Northern Ireland bank notes are not legal tender anywhere, although many shops accept them. Jersey, Guernsey, and Isle of Man notes and coins are legal tender only on those islands. Fifty pence, 25p and 20p coins are legal tender up to £10. Ten pence and 5p coins are legal tender up to £5. Two pence and 1p coins are legal tender up to 20p. This means that shopkeepers can, if they wish, refuse to accept 22p or more in penny and twopenny coins, and ask for larger denominations instead. Shopkeepers are also not required by law to give change, and strictly speaking, cannot be forced to give change. It is up to the person making the offer to pay the exact amount.

Ownership of Goods

Once a contract has been made (see above) the title, or ownership of the goods, changes hands, regardless of whether or not any money has been paid. This means that if a customer makes an *offer* to buy an article, and you *accept* the offer, and he says that he will be back later to pay for it, the customer is now the owner of the article, and the shopkeeper has no right to put that article back into his stock or to sell it because it no longer belongs to him. He does, however, have a 'lien' on it, which means that he is entitled to hold on to it until he has been paid. But once the article physically changes hands the lien is lost and he has no rights to repossess it. If the goods are perishable, and the customer does not return within a reasonable time to pay for them, the shopkeeper may sell them, although he is technically selling goods that do not belong to him. In order to avoid this situation the shopkeeper should make it clear to the customer, either verbally or by having it printed on his order forms and invoices, etc., that the goods will remain his property until paid for in full. This means that if someone pays by cheque, and the cheque bounces, the shopkeeper will be entitled to call round and take back the article in question. The right of lien also extends to repairs. If a customer brings in an article for repair, you are entitled to hold on to that article until the repair bill has been paid, regardless of how valuable the article is.

Deposits

Whether or not deposits are refundable is a very difficult question. Many things which we call deposits are not really deposits at all. There are three types of 'deposit':

(1) *Holding deposit* This is when a customer asks you to keep an item for him until such time as he comes in to buy it. In this case the deposit is to stop you from selling it to someone else, and if he changes his mind, he is not entitled to a refund. He has simply paid you a sum of money to stop anyone else from buying it. In fact, if he does decide to buy the article, he should then pay the full price in addition to any holding deposit he has already paid.

(2) *Part payment* This is when a customer agrees to buy something, pays a certain amount, and tells you he will pay the balance when he collects it.

(3) *Combination holding deposit/part payment* This is the most common form, and is simply a combination of (1) and (2). In both (1) and (2) the customer is not entitled to a refund if he has deprived the retailer of making a profit. For instance, if the article put aside is one of hundreds in stock and no loss in sales has ensued, the customer is entitled to a refund. But if the retailer has lost sales by not being able to offer the article for sale, the customer is not entitled to a refund. What is more, the retailer is fully justified in asking the customer to pay him the difference between the deposit and the amount of profit he would have made if he had been able to sell the article. If the customer refused to pay this amount, the retailer could sue him.

The safest way is to ask the customer if he agrees with whichever type of deposit you are willing to accept. Once he does this, a verbal contract will have been made. If a proviso has been included in the order, such as, 'I will have one if you can get it by Monday', and you cannot supply by Monday, then you will have to return the deposit.

Uncollected Goods

If you run a service and have uncollected goods you can dispose of them in accordance with the Torts (Interference with Goods) Act 1977. This allows the retailer to demand payment or to sell the article providing the following procedures have been followed. First of all you must send a letter by recorded or registered post to the customer's last known address (it does not matter if he does not live there anymore), and set out in detail a description of the goods, the work that has been carried out, the date they were brought in, the date they were ready for collection, the amount owing, and the date they will be sold if not collected. This date must be at least three months after the date the notice was sent. If there is no response to this letter you may sell the item(s) by whatever means are most appropriate and for any amount. Any balance of money left after deducting the amount owed to you should be kept for the customer to collect at a later date. If this sum of money has not been claimed after six years, you may keep it. To comply with the Act you have to send the letter, so make sure you *always* ask for the customer's address when you accept an item. There is no need to display a notice about non-collection.

Supply of Goods Acts

The law states that with any sales you make, the goods must:

(a) correspond with the description;
(b) be of merchantable quality;
(c) be fit for the purpose.

(a) 'Correspond with the description.' The goods must be as described. It does not matter whether you give an oral description of them, or whether the customer selects something by himself from the information given on the label, packaging or shelf. For instance, 'Size 2 Free Range Eggs' must be size 2 and be free range.
(b) 'Of merchantable quality.' The goods must be as fit for the purpose as it is reasonable to expect, taking into account the description applied to them, the price, and any other relevant information. For instance, if you bought a new kettle you would not expect the handle to fall off after a few days of use; but if you bought a five year old motor bike you should not expect it to perform like a new motor bike, although you should expect the same kind of performance that you would get from an average bike with that mileage.
(c) 'Fit for the purpose.' If you are asked for goods for a particular purpose, they must be reasonably fit for that purpose. For example, if you are asked for a rivet extractor for a motor bike chain and you supply one that will only work on a bicycle chain, you will have to refund the money or supply another that will work on a motor bike.

If goods do not correspond with (a), (b) or (c) above, the customer is entitled to a cash refund. He does not have to accept a credit note and may even have a claim for losses or expenses subsequently incurred.

Points to remember A customer is not entitled to a refund owing to defects if these are specifically pointed out before the sale. Likewise, no refund is due for obvious defects if the customer has examined the goods before buying them. If there is something wrong, it is only the *buyer* who can complain, not, for example, the person who received it as a present. If a person changes his mind about an item, perhaps about the colour, you do not have to do anything at all. You do not have to give a refund if the article has been damaged through not following the instructions. Regarding 'fit for the purpose', if you are asked a question about an item and you make it clear that you do not know if it will be suitable, the customer has no redress if he decides to buy it.

Late Date Goods

It is *not* an offence to sell goods after the 'sell by' or 'best before' dates. It *is* an offence to sell goods which are not of merchantable quality, regardless of the date on them. The difference is that if the product is sold and found to be of inedible quality before the date, the manufacturer is ultimately responsible, and if it is after the date, the shopkeeper is responsible. It makes no difference if you label or describe the goods as 'late date' or offer them for sale at a special low price. This is not a problem if a little common sense is used. For instance, a can of beer that originally had a 12 month life is hardly likely to taste any different a month out of code, but a pot of cream that originally had a four day life could not be trusted three days later. Many factors have to be taken into consideration when deciding how long to sell an item of food after the date has elapsed, but no problems should be encountered if the original length of life is considered along with the way in which the goods have been stored. Obviously the pot of cream would be fine for weeks after the date if it had been frozen before the expiry date and offered for sale in a frozen condition.

Food hygiene regulations These regulations are enforced by the Local Authority Health Department and cover the premises, the protection of food from contamination, and personal hygiene and health.

Registering and Licensing

Milk If you sell milk, you should be registered with the local authority.

Ice-cream If you sell ice-cream you should be registered with the local authority.

Poisons Under the Poisons Act 1972 a licence is needed to sell poisons. As an example, some hair colourants and disinfectants contain poison, also weedkillers, etc.

Children

It is an offence to sell a pet to a child under 12 years of age.
It is an offence to sell cigarettes to a child under 16 years of age.
It is an offence to sell fireworks to a child under 16 years of age.
It is an offence to sell lottery tickets to a child under 16 years of age.

A child under 10 cannot be charged with any criminal offence.
From aged 10 to under 17 a child can be charged with a criminal offence before a juvenile court.
At 17 he appears in an adult court.

Firework Regulations

(1) The maximum fine for selling fireworks to under 16 year olds is £2,000.
(2) The maximum amount of fireworks you can store in your shop is 250kg.
(3) Up to 50kg can be kept in metal containers, cupboards, wooden boxes, or glass showcases, which should be locked.
(4) If your stock is more than 50kg it must be kept in closed metal containers, each holding no more than 50kg. This does not include shop display stock.
(5) You may keep up to 1,000kg of shop goods fireworks in a safe and secure building used exclusively for that purpose.
(6) You must not keep more than 50kg of fireworks in a room to which the public have access.
(7) You must not place glass display cases in shop windows.
(8) You must not keep any other articles in a container that is being used for the storage of fireworks.
(9) Make sure *your* fireworks are stored in a dry place.
(10) Label the containers 'Fireworks'.
(11) Make sure no one smokes near display cases or containers.
(12) Fireworks cannot be sold until three weeks before 5 November.

CHAPTER 12

Reference Section

Small Firms Service

The Small Firms Service is run by the Department of Trade and Industry and can be of great help to anyone thinking of buying a shop, as well as to those who already run a business. They produce a series of useful free booklets, and can be contacted on the telephone by dialling 100 and asking for Freefone 2444. If you wish to visit one of their Centres for advice, it is advisable to telephone the Freefone number first, because some Centres are due to be re-located. If you wish, you may write to the address below instead:

    Small Firms Division
    Department of Trade and Industry
    Ashdown House
    123 Victoria Street
    London SW1E 6RB

The Manpower Services Commission

The Manpower Services Commission will give details of various courses and schemes available. Look in your local telephone directory for the number to ring, or call in at your nearest Job Centre.

College Courses

College Courses leading to Diplomas and Certificates are offered by the College for the Distributive Trades, 30 Leicester Square, London WC2H 7LE. Tel. 01 839 1547. Details of courses available and entry requirements may be obtained from the college.

Colleges of Further Education

Colleges of Further Education sometimes offer various courses and seminars which may prove useful. Contact those within easy distance and ask for details.

Voluntary Associations

The Head Office of many of the Voluntary Associations is given below.

Fotovalue
276 Chase Road, Southgate, London N14 6HA. Tel. 01 882 2011.

Jivandas Buying Group
Jivandas House, 1–7 Garman Road, Tottenham, London N17. Tel. 01 801 9499.

Londis
Eurogroup House, 67/71 High Street, Hampton Hill, Middx. TW12 1LZ. Tel. 01 941 0344.

Mace Line
Gerrards House, Station Road, Gerrards Cross, Bucks, SL9 8HW. Tel. 0753 887355.

Spar (UK)
32-40 Headstone Drive, Harrow, Middx. HA3 5QT. Tel. 01 863 5511.

Maid Marian
Danish Bacon, Howardsgate, Welwyn Garden City, Herts. Tel. 07073 23421.

N.I.S.A. Ltd
(National Independent Supermarkets Association) PO Box 45, Rotherham, S60 5BY. Tel. 0709 782589.

Numark Chemist Group
51 Boreham Road, Warminster, Wilts. BA12 9JU. Tel. 0985 215555.

Topdec
(Wallpaper, paint etc.) PGW Holdings Ltd., Chilton House, Station Road, Chesham, Bucks. Tel 0494 774311.

Unichem
(chemists) Cox Lane, Chessington, Surrey. Tel. 01 391 2323.

VG Distributors Ltd
PO Box 58, Charter Avenue, Canley, Coventry, CV4 8AD. Tel. 0203 465200

Vantage Chemists
West Lane, Runcorn, Cheshire, WA7 2PE. Tel. 0928 717070.

Vikas Buying Group
17–19 Grove Vale, East Dulwich, London, SC22 8EQ. Tel. 01 693 4175.

Some More Useful Addresses

Association of Certified & Corporate Accountants
22 Bedford Square, London WC13 3HS.

Association of British Chambers of Commerce
6-14 Dean Farrar Street, London SW1H 0DX.

British Insurance Brokers' Association
Fountain House, 130 Fenchurch Street, London EC3M 5DJ. Tel. 01 623 9043.

Business Education Council
76 Portland Place, London W1.

Council for Small Industries in Rural Areas (COSIRA)
141 Castle Street, Salisbury, Wilts. SP1 3TP. Tel. (0722) 336255.

Department of Employment
22 St James's Square, London SW1 4JB.

Institute of Chartered Accountants
Moorgate Place, London EC2P 2BJ. Tel. 01 628 7060.

Royal Institute of Chartered Surveyors
12 Great George Street, Parliament Square, London SW1P 3AD.

Society of Company and Commercial Accountants
11 Portland Road, Edgbaston, Birmingham, B16 9HN.

Office of Fair Trading
Field House, 15/25 Breams Buildings, London EC4 1PR. Tel. 01 242 2858.

Law Society
113 Chancery Lane, London W1. Tel. 01 242 1222.

Royal Institute of British Architects
66 Portland Place, London W1N 4AB. Tel. 01 580 5533.

Trade Associations

There follows a list of the main Trade Associations, many of which produce a trade journal. These can provide some valuable sources of information.

Amalgamated Master Dairymen Ltd
Bradford & Bingley House, 220 Hoe Street, London E17 3AY. Tel. 01 521 8855.

Association of British Laundry, Cleaning & Rental Services Ltd
Lancaster Gate House, 319 Pinner Road, Harrow. Tel. 01 863 7755.

Association Of Independent Retailers
Newton Road, Worcester WR5 1JX. Tel. 0905 28165.

Bakery Allied Traders Associated Ltd
6 Catherine Street, London WC2B 5JJ. Tel. 01 836 2460.

Bookmakers Association
22 Malthouse Lane, Birmingham, B8. Tel. 021 327 3031.

Booksellers Association of Great Britain and Ireland
154 Buckingham Palace Road, London SW1W 9TZ. Tel. 01 730 8214.

British Antique Dealers Association
20 Rutland Gate, London SW7 1BD. Tel. 01 589 4128.

British Franchise Association
Franchise Chambers, 75a Bell Street, Henley on Thames, Oxon. Tel. 0491 578049.

British Fur Trade Association
68 Upper Thames Street, London EC4V 3AN. Tel. 01 248 5947.

British Hardware Federation
20 Harborne Rd, Edgbaston, Birmingham B15 3AB. Tel. 021 454 4385.

British Hotels, Restaurants and Caterers Association
40 Duke Street, London W1M 6HR. Tel. 01 499 6641.

British Independent Grocers Association (BIGA)
Federation House, 17 Farnborough Street, Farnborough, Hants. GU14 8AG (F515001)

British Jewellery & Giftware Federation
27 Frederick Street, Brimingham B1 3HJ. Tel. 021 236 2657.

British Retailers Association
Commonwealth House, 1/19 New Oxford Street, London WC1A 1PA. Tel. 01 404 0955.

Consumer Credit Association of the United Kingdom
Queens House, Queens Road, Chester CH1 3BQ. Tel. 0244 312044.

Consumer Credit Trade Association
3 Berners Street, London W1P 3AG. Tel. 01 636 7564.

Delicatessen and Fine Food Association
3 Fairfield Avenue, Staines, Middx. TW18 4AB. Tel. 0784 61339.

Drapers' Chamber of Trade
North Bar, Banbury, Oxon. Tel. 0295 53601.

Federation of Sports Goods Distributors Ltd
7 Pelham Road, Lindfield, Haywards Heath, Sussex RH16 2EW. Tel. 04447 3769.

Food and Drink Federation
6 Catherine Street, London WC2 5JJ. Tel. 01 836 2460.

Footwear Distributors' Federation
Commonwealth House, 1/19 New Oxford Street, London WC1A 1PA. Tel. 01 404 0955.

Horticultural Trades Association
19 High St, Theale, Reading, Berks RG7 5AH. Tel. 0734 303132.

Independent Footwear Retailers Association
3 Masons Avenue, Wealdstone, Harrow HA3 5AH. Tel. 01 427 1545.

Institute of Meat
Boundary House, 91/93 Charterhouse Street, London EC1M 6HR. Tel. 01 253 2971.

London Fish & Poultry Retailers Association
66 Aberdour Rd, Goodmayes, Essex IG3 9PG. Tel. 01 590 4200.

Menswear Association of Britain Ltd
Palladium House,1-4 Argyll St, London W1V 2HR. Tel. 01 734 6865.

Music Trades Association
PO Box 249, London W4 5EX. Tel. 01 994 7592.

National Association of Cycle & Motor Cycle Traders Ltd
31a High St, Tunbridge Wells, Kent TN1 1XN. Tel. 0892 26081.

National Association of Health Stores
Byron House, 1 College St, Nottingham, Notts. NG1 5AQ. Tel. 0602 474165.

National Association of Master Bakers, Confectioners & Caterers
50 Alexandra Rd, Wimbledon SW19 7BR. Tel. 01 947 7781.

National Association of Retail Furnishers
17-21 George St, Croydon CR9 1TQ. Tel. 01 680 8444.

National Association of Shopfitters
NAS House, 411 Limpsfield Rd, The Green, Warlingham, Surrey CR3 9HA. Tel. 088 32 4961.

National Association of Shopkeepers
Lynch House, 91 Mansfield Rd, Nottingham, Notts NG1 3FN. Tel. 0602 475046.

National Association of Toy Retailers
20 Knave Wood Rd, Kemsing, Sevenoaks, Kent.

National Chamber of Trade
Enterprise House, Henley on Thomas, Oxon. RG9 1TU. Tel. 0491 576161.

National Federation of Fish Friers
Federation House, 289 Dewsbury Rd, Leeds LS11 5HW. Tel. 0532 713291.

National Federation of Fishmongers Ltd
Queensway House, 2 Queensway, Redhill, Surrey RH1 1QS. Tel. Redhill 68611.

National Federation of Meat Traders
1 Belgrove, Tunbridge Wells, Kent.

National Federation of Retail Newsagents
2 Bridewell Place, London EC4 6AR. Tel. 01 353 6816.

National Federation of Subpostmasters
Evelyn House, 22 Windlesham Gdns, Shoreham by Sea BN4 5AZ. Tel. 07917 2324.

National Hairdressers Federation
11 Goldington Rd, Bedford MK40 3JY. Tel. 0234 60332.

National Institute of Hardware
10 Leam Terrace, Leamington Spa. Tel. Leamington Spa 21284.

The National Pharmaceutical Association Ltd
Mallinson House, 40–42 St. Peter's St, St Albans, Herts AL1 3NP. Tel. 0727 32161.

National Union of Licensed Victuallers
2 Downing St, Farnham, Surrey GU9 7NX. Tel. 0252 714448.

Office Machines & Equipment Federation.
16 Wood St, Kingston-upon-Thames, Surrey KT1 1UE. Tel. 01 549 7699.

The Pet Trade Association Ltd
151 Pampisford Rd, South Croydon, Surrey CR2 6DE. Tel. 01 681 3708.

Radio, Electrical & Television Retailers Association
Retra House, 57–61 Newington Causeway, London SE1 6BE. Tel. 01 403 1463.

Retail Confectioners & Tobacconists Association Ltd
Ashley House, 53 Christchurch Ave, London N12 0DH. Tel. 01 445 6344.

Retail Fruit Trade Federation
108/110 Market Towers, Nine Elms Lane, London SW8 5NS. Tel. 01 720 9168.

Shop & Display Equipment Association
24 Croydon Rd, Caterham, Surrey CR3 6YR. Tel. 0883 48911.

Society of Master Shoe Repairers
St. Crispin's House, 21 Station Rd, Desborough, Northants NN14 2SA. Tel. 0536 760374.

Wallpaper, Paint & Wallcovering Retailers Association
PO Box 44, Walshall, West Midlands, Tel. 0922 31134.

Trade Journals

As well as journals published by Trade Associations there are a multitude of others that can be obtained from your newsagent. Some of these are listed below. There are also a number of free magazines available to those already in business.

Antiques Trade Gazette
Bookseller
Caterer and Hotelkeeper
Chemist and Druggist
Drapers' Record
CTN/Confectioner, Tobacconist & Confectioner
Fast Foodservice
Fish Trader
Fruit Trades Journal

The Grocer
Hairdressers Journal International
Hardware Trade Journal
Meat Trades Journal
Newsagent
Painting and Decorating Journal
Retail Newsagent Tobacconist & Confectioner
Show and Leather News
Video Retailer

Up-to-date information on employment law can be obtained either from your local Jobcentre, or from any of the regional offices of ACAS (Advisory, Conciliation and Arbitration Service) listed below.

Northern Region
Westgate House, Westgate Road, Newcastle upon Tyne, NE1 1TJ. Tel. 0632 612191

Yorkshire and Humberside Region
Commerce House, St. Albans Place, Leeds, LS2 8HH. Tel. 0532 431371

South East Region
Clifton House, 83 Euston Road, London, NW1 2RB. Tel. 01 388 5100

London Region
Clifton House, 83 Euston Road, London, NW1 2RB. Tel. 01 388 5100

South West Region
16 Park Place, Clifton, Bristol, BS8 1JP. Tel. 0272 211921

Midlands Region
Alpha Tower, Suffolk Street Queensway, Birmingham, B1 1TZ. Tel. 021 643 9911

Nottingham Sub-office, 66 Houndsgate, Nottingham, NG1 6BA. Tel. 0602 415450

North West Region
Boulton House, 17 Chorlton Street, Manchester, M1 3HY. Tel. 061 228 3222
Merseyside Sub-office, Cressington House, 249 St. Mary's Road, Garston, Liverpool, L19 0NF. Tel. 051 427 8881/4

Scotland
Franborough House, 123 Bothwell Street, Glasgow, G2 7JR. Tel. 041 204 2677

Wales
Phase 1, Ty Glas Road, Llanishen, Cardiff, CF4 5PH. Tel. 0222 762 636

THE CLEAR 'n' EASY TRADERS YEARLY ACCOUNTS BOOK

[EXAMPLE SHEET]

Keep tabs on your business with this new simplified design of traders yearly accounts book which has been produced with the help of Customs and Excise.

Banish your paperwork headaches — using this accounts book is as easy as ABC. So easy, in fact, that anyone can understand it. Even the quarterly VAT return can be completed in a matter of minutes. It could also help to reduce your accountant's fees!

Everything is clearly laid out. One page for one week. Shows details of daily takings, other receipts, banking, space if required for sales subject to VAT, goods purchased for resale, trade expenses subject to VAT, trade expenses not subject to VAT, current bank balance, total amounts paid out during the week in cash and cheques, and also shows how much cash you should have in hand at the end of the week. Clear and precise instructions for using the book are printed inside the front cover, and an example sheet is included.

The accounts book measures 14″ × 10″, covers a whole year's trading, and is very realistically priced at only £5.98 including VAT and post and packing.

Copies may be obtained from Peter Levene,

43 The Cliff, Roedean, Brighton, BN2 5RF.

Please make cheques payable to P. Levene. Money refunded in full if not delighted.

Index

'A' Boards, 6
A/C payee only, 102
ACAS, 136, 151
Acceptance (contracts), 139
Accidents in the shop, 137
Accountants, 115, 116
Accounts books, 109
Adjustors, 108
Advertisements, 64
Advice, 117
Agencies, 31
Agreements, 124
Alarm systems, 97
Alcohol by volume, 70
Alcohol-free drinks, 69
Alertness, 94
Alternatives, 38
Ambiguous prices, 89
American statistics, 90
Annual shrinkage, 90
Appearances, 1
Apprehending customers, 91
Assessors, 108
Assigning leases, 120
'Averaging', 106

Back-dated wage claims, 125
Back-up fridges, 79
Bacon, 52–56
Bacteria, 78
Bags, 61, 85
Bank balances, 104
   charges, 103, 104
   Holidays, 25
   interest, 102
   loans, 102
   managers, 102, 123
   notes, 140
Bankers cards, 86

Banking, 98, 102–105
   private a/c's, 104
Base rate, 102
Baskets, 89, 90
Bedsitters, 32
Beefburgers, 59
'Best before', 143
Best sellers, 25
Bleaching cloths, 49
Boarding-up, 95
Books, secondhand, 32
Bookwork, 109, 117–120
Borrowing money, 102
Bottles, 7
Boxes
   displaying, 22
   opening, 23
Breakages, 137
Break-ins, 2, 94–97
Breaking agreements, 124
British standards, 73
Brokers, 108
Building societies, 105
Bulk waste containers, 7
Burglar alarms, 97
Butter, 44
Buy locally, 21
Buying a shop, 116, 120–125

Calculators, 100, 114
Calor gas, 31
Cameras, 93
Canvassing, 63
Capital Gains Tax, 121
Car insurance, 107
Carded goods, 25
Cash, 88, 98
Cash & Carry, 21
Cash balance, 110

INDEX

counting, 88
payments, 104–110
refunds, 142
registers, 10, 13
shortages, 85
'Casing the joint', 121
Cats, 5, 111
Ceilings, 4
Chain reactions, 25
Change, 140
Charity raffle, 27
Checking invoices, 118
Checkout errors, 84
Checkouts, 88, 93
Cheese, 44–46
  cutting, 45
  displaying, 45
  life, 44
  temperature, 44
  types, 45
Cheeseboards, 46
Cheeseburgers, 59
Cheque books, 103
Cheques, 40, 86, 104
  a/c payee, 102
  bankers cards, 40, 86, 104
  bounced, 87
  'not negotiable', 102
  single, 87
  small, 104
  stolen, 87
  unpaid, 104
  unsigned, 40
  writing, 102, 103
Children, 88, 90, 130, 143
  cigarettes, 143
  criminal offences, 143
  employing, 130
  fireworks, 144
  lottery tickets, 143
  pets, 143
Chilled cabinets, 77–79
Chilled foods, 78
Christmas
  afterwards, 28
  club receipts, 110
  decorations, 5, 50
  gifts, 83
  hampers, 28
  insurance, 71
  parties, 83
  stock, 28
Cider, 69
Cigarettes, 13, 14, 143
Claiming on insurance, 107

Cleaning
  cloths, 49
  equipment, 6
  glass, 6
  sinks, 49
  tickets, 49
Cleaning and Hygiene, 6, 49, 50
Clear 'n' Easy, 109, 110, 153
Cling film, 45
Clock repairs, 31
Closing the sale, 39
Clotted cream, 44
Coffee, 59
Coffee machines, 59
Coins, 140
Cold drinks, 28
Cold room, 28
Collecting debts, 40
Collections, 34
College courses, 145
Colleges of Further Education, 145
Colour coding, 88
Combined Insurance Policies, 105
Complaining, 119
Complaints, 39
Compost, 31
Computer print-outs, 118
Computer statements, 115
Consideration (contract), 139
Consumer Protection Act 1987, 138
Contempt of court, 124
Contingency plans, 82
Contract of Employment, 125, 131
Contracts, 11
  sale of goods, 140
  service, 9
Cooked gammon, 56
Cooked meats, 46, 48, 78
Copy of lease, 124
Correspond with description, 142
Cost of wrappings, 23, 52
Costs, 110
Counting in 5's and 6's, 100
Crates, 7
Cream, 44
Credit, 40, 63
  cards, 111
  information agencies, 94
  notes, 142
  terms, 104, 117
Crime prevention, 97, 98
Criminal records, 135
Customer appearance, 36
  apprehending, 91
  complaints, 39

credit, 40, 41
collusion, 85
debts, 40
eating in shop, 91
obnoxious, 36
offers, 41
orders, 24, 35, 139
problems, 39
receipts, 13
relations, 36
requests, 39
stealing, 89
waiting, 37
Cutting foods, 48

Dairy cabinets, 79
Dairy facts, 43
Damaged goods, 91
Damages
  sued for, 137
Dark spots, 96
Dates, 143
Debts, 40
Decisions, 8
Deductions, 85
Defects, 142
Defrost cycle, 75
Defrosting freezers, 76
Delayed reactions, 25
Delicatessen counters, 50
Delicatessens, 43
Deliveries, 34, 35, 37
Delivery
  costs, 10
  men, 33-35
  notes, 118
Deposits, 23, 140, 141
Deterrents, 92, 97
Different ways of selling, 27
Discounts, 33, 51
Disinfectants, 143
Dismissal, 132
Display equipment, 61, 77
Displaying goods, 22, 23, 77
Displaying prices, 137
Dogs, 5, 97, 111
Door frames, 96
Doors, 3, 95
Double cream, 44
Drainpipes, 95
Drinking on premises, 69
Drunks, 68, 69
Dry cleaning, 31
Dump bins, 26
Dustmen, 7

Eating in shop, 91
Economising, 52
Edam, 45
Electric cables, 14
Electricity
  saving, 12, 76, 79
Employer's liability, 108
Employment
  ages, 130
  Bill, 130
  terms and conditions, 131
End pieces, 32
Engaging staff, 80
Enthusiasm, 37, 51
Equal Pay Acts, 130
Equipment
  buying, 9
  display, 6, 34
  guarantees, 10
  moving, 12
  reconditioned, 10
Estimates, 1
Exotic foods, 27, 62
Expenses, 111-114
Extra sales, 38
Extractor fans, 76

Facings, 25, 29, 76
Fans, 76
Fast foods, 58
Father's Day, 28
Features, 37
Filing, 109, 118
Filled rolls, 51
Fingerprints, 96
Fingers, 50
Fire
  extinguishers, 14
  insurance, 14
  precautions, 13
Fireworks, 144
First loss, 13
First year profits, 116
'Fit for the purpose', 142
Fixed fee interviews, 136
Fixed rate loans, 102
Flat roofs, 95
Floating rates, 102
Floats, 88
Floor space, 7
Flooring, 3
Fluorescent tubes, 4, 5
Food Hygiene Regulations, 143
Food Labelling Regulations, 46

Free
  deliveries, 37
  offers, 138
Freehold shops, 123
Freezers, 72-79
  British Standards, 73
  breakdowns, 77
  defrosting, 76
  displays, 72
  open/closed, 73
  temperatures, 75, 77
Freezing food, 74
Fresh foods, 22
Fresh food image, 79
Fridges, 77-79
Front door, 3
Frozen food, 74
Fruit and vegetables, 60-63
'Full and final settlement', 108
Future alternatives, 43
Future of area, 123

Getaway vehicles, 97
Giro, 98, 104
Giving change, 140
Glass, 6
  counters, 6, 78
  windows, 95
Gondolas, 8
Goods
  defects, 142
  in short supply, 24
  in transit, 107
  ownership, 140
  returned, 142
  uncollected, 141
Graphs, 111-112
Greengrocers, 60-63
Greetings cards, 64
Grocers, 42-43
  guidelines, 42
Gross profit, 15, 113
Guarantees, 10
Guernsey coins, 140
Gunpowder, 70

Hair colourants, 143
Half cream, 44
Ham, 46, 56
Hampers, 28
Handling cash, 98
Happy shop, 37
Health
  and beauty, 31
  foods, 79
  insurance, 108
  Regulations, 6, 46
Heating in shops, 136
Hidden cameras, 93
High profit lines, 25, 38
Hinges, 96
Hire purchase, 11
Hiring out
  equipment, 31
  drinks machines, 59
'Holding deposits', 141
Holidays, 38
Home
  consumption, 112, 113
  cooked gammon, 46, 56
  medicines, 31
Homogonised milk, 44
Hot
  air, 75
  weather, 75
Hours
  licensing, 68
  shop, 13, 25
  staff, 82

Ice-cream, 74, 75, 143
Improvements, 2
In store bakeries, 57-58
Increasing sales, 25-27
Industrial tribunals, 135
Infectious behaviour, 29
Information, 119
Injunctions, 124
Instant print, 43
Instruction manuals, 10
Insurance, 14, 71, 105-108
  adjustors, 108
  arguments, 108
  assessors, 108
  averaging, 106
  brokers, 108
  car, 107
  claiming, 107
  combined policies, 105
  conditions, 107
  disputes, 108
  employer's liability, 108
  full and final settlement, 108
  goods in cars, 107
  health, 108
  'material facts', 106
  policies, 105, 106
  stock value, 106
  theft, 107
Interest, 102
Interviewing, 80

Intestate, 126
Investment accounts, 104
Invoices
  checking, 118
  filing, 118
Isle of Man notes and coins, 140
Itemised pay statements, 132

Jersey coins, 140
Jury
  service, 129
  staff, 129

Knives
  sharp, 48
  using, 48
Knowledge, 51

Laminated glass, 95
Landlords, 124
  permission, 2, 120
Large stores, 89
Larger sizes, 30
Late date goods, 26, 143
Law
  queries, 136
  of contracts, 139
'Leakers', 22
Leasehold shops, 123
Leases
  assigning, 120
  copies, 124
  end of, 127
  revisions, 127
Leasing agreements, 11
Leaves, 61
Legal fees, 121
Legal tender, 140
Letter boxes, 96
Licences, 43
Licensing hours, 68
Licking fingers, 50
Lien, 140
Lighting, 4, 50
Linked sales, 38
Load lines, 74
Loans, 102
Local events, 6
Local promotions, 27
Locks, 96
Loss adjustors, 108
  assessors, 108
  relief, 116
Lottery tickets, 32, 143
Low alcohol drinks, 69

Making decisions, 8
Manana, 50
Manpower Services Commission, 145
Manufacturer's Recommended Price, 138
Margarine, 44
'Material facts', 106
Meat, 46
  slicers, 49
  slicing, 48–49
Medicines, 31
Melons, 51
Merchandising, 23, 35, 51
'Merchantable quality', 142
Mess, 110
Messages, 35
Metal shutters, 2
Method of three, 91
Microwave ovens, 59–60
Milk, 18, 43–44, 143
  homogonised, 44
  pasteurised, 43
  semi-skimmed, 44
  skimmed, 44
  sterilised, 44
  UHT, 44
Misleading the public, 137
Money-off coupons, 118
Money-saving, 12–13
Monitors, 93
Mothers Day, 28
Music, 5

Nameplates, 10
National Insurance, 83
Negligence, 137
Net profit, 42, 94
New car/fridge, etc, 113
  customers, 125
  faces, 92, 125
  features, 37
  lines, 30, 51
  shopstaff, 125
Newsagents, 63–64
Newspaper ads, 66
Newspaper deliveries, 63
Night covers, 76
Norms, 42
Northern Ireland Banknotes, 140
'Not negotiable', 102
Notice boards, 6, 81

Objections, 39
Off licences, 66–71
Offers (contract), 139, 140
Offices and Shops Act, 136

INDEX

Open food, 46
Opening tins, 46
Opportunities, 83
Opposition, 30
Order sheets, 21
Ordering, 21, 33, 34
Orders
 proof, 35
Original gravity, 70
Other shops, 30
Outers, 22
Overcharging, 92
Overdrafts, 105
Ownership of goods, 140

Painting, 3
Paper bags, 23
Paper boys, 63
Part payment, 141
Part-time, 83
Partnerships (tax), 116
Passwords, 91
Pasteurised milk, 43
Paying in advance, 33
Payment in lieu of notice, 83
Payment of legal fees, 121
Payphones, 12
Pensions, 108–109
Percentage of profit, 15–19
Performing Rights Society, 5
Personnel, 129
Petrol, 110
Petrol stations, 43
Pets, 111, 143
Phone cards, 106
Photocopiers, 24, 64
Photographic processing, 31
Photographs, 93, 137
Planning officer, 123
Planning permission, 1
Plants, 31
Plastic bags, 61
Plastic tickets, 49
Pockets, 88
Poisons Act 1972, 143
Polystyrene cups, 59
Position of stock, 29, 30
Post Office Giro, 98, 104
Post Office salary units, 117
Posters, 6
Pot Noodles, 59
Potential trade, 43
Premises, 94
Prepacking, 19–20, 23
Prepricing, 20

Price
 ambiguous, 89
 comparisons, 37
 flashed products, 19
 increases, 139
 lists, 75
Pricing
 goods, 137, 139
 guns, 22
 more than one ticket, 139
 policies, 25–27
 tickets, 139
 upwards, 139
Private a/c's, 104
Procrastination, 109
Profit margins, 15–19
Profit on return, 15
Projected accounts, 114
Promotions, 51
 and pricing, 25–27
Proof
 of orders, 35
 of shoplifting, 92
 spirit, 70
Property improvements, 2
Protection Orders, 67
Psychology, 29

Race Relations Act, 130
Raffles, 27
Rationalisation, 30
Ready reckoner, 18
'Reasonableness', 134
Reasons for selling shops, 122–123
Receipts
 customers, 12
 goods, 34
 work done, 3
Recommended Retail Price, 138
Reconditioned equipment, 10
Recorded delivery, 119
Redundancy, 132–133
 pay, 132
 table, 133
Reference section, 145–153
Refrigerated counters, 49
Refrigeration, 72–79
Refunds, 142
Registering, 143
Rent
 arrears, 121
 revisions, 127
Repairs, 141
Representatives, 33–35
 messages, 35

Requesting information, 119
Reserve stock, 96
Restrictive covenants, 124–125
Retirement, 116
    Capital Gains Tax, 121
    staff, 130
Return on investment, 121–122
'Returns', 117
Right of lien, 140
Right of refusal, 92
Rights, 140
Roofs, 95

Safe places, 118
Safes, 98
Sale or return, 34
Sales
    extra, 38
    linked, 38
    reductions, 139
    representatives, 33
Samples, 51
Sandwich deliveries, 32
Sandwiches, 32, 58
Saving money, 12–13
Scales, 6, 10
School uniforms, 31
Scottish Bank Notes, 140
Seasonal lines, 28, 38
Secondhand
    books, 32
    equipment, 10
Security, 2, 105
    cameras, 84
    customers, 40
    deterrents, 92, 97
    walks, 14
Seeds, 31
'Sell-by' dates, 46, 78, 143
Selling
    a shop, 116, 120
    goods, 36–39
Semi-skimmed milk, 44
Sequential sales, 25
Serve-overs
    lighting, 50
Service contracts, 9
Serving, 37–39
Sex discrimination, 129
Shelving, 5, 29
Shoe repairs, 31
Shop
    heating, 136
    hours, 13
    left empty, 98
    package insurance, 105
    premises, 94
    selling, 120
    temperatures, 3
Shopfronts, 1, 95
Shoplifting, 89–94
Short-dated goods, 26
Short supply, 24
Shrinkage, 90
Shutters, 2
Signs, 6
Single cheques, 87
Single cream, 44
Sinks, 49
Skimmed milk, 44
Skylights, 95
Slicers, 6, 49
Slicing by hand, 48
Slow moving lines, 29, 99
Small
    bottles, 93
    cheques, 104
    claims, 87, 94
    Firms Service, 145
    goods, 93
Smaller sizes, 30
Smile, 29, 36
Smoking, 13
Soft drinks, 28
Sole traders, 116
Solicitors, 136
Soup, 59
Spare cheque books, 103
Spare parts, 9
Special presentation, 87
Special requests, 39
'Spent convictions', 135
Spirits, 93
Spot checks, 84
Spot lights, 4
Staff
    appraisal 81
    bags, 85
    cash shortages, 85
    Christmas gifts, 83
    collusion, 85
    contingency plans, 82
    contracts, 131
    criminal records, 135
    deductions, 85
    dismissal, 132, 134
    educating, 85
    employers liability, 108
    engaging, 80
    holidays, 82

INDEX

hours, 82
in new shop, 125
income tax, 83
interviews, 80
Maternity Pay, 131
National Insurance, 83
notice, 132, 134
own goods, 85
part-time, 83, 135
security, 83
sickness, 82
spot checks, 84
suspicions, 81
tests, 81
time off, 82
till errors, 84
under, 18, 68, 130
underringing, 84
unfair dismissal, 134
uniforms, 81
unusual actions, 84
value of, 80
wages, 82, 131
wastage, 29, 82
working conditions, 136
Stains, 4
State pensions, 109
Stationery, 64
Statistics, 90
Statutory Maternity Pay, 131
Statutory Sick Pay, 131
Stealing, 89–94
  apprehending, 91
  children, 88, 90
  deterrents, 92–94
  large stores, 89
  new faces, 92
  proof, 92
  quiet times, 91
Steel doors, 95
Sterilised milk, 44
Stock, 21–22
  different types, 106
  figures, 99–101
  larger sizes, 30
  levels, 101
  position, 29, 30
  reducing, 21
  rotation, 20
  slow movers, 29, 99
  smaller sizes, 30
  value, insurance, 106
Stockroom, 20
Stocktakers, 99, 101
Stocktaking, 99–101

form, 100
Stolen cheques, 87
Storage of goods, 20
Sugar, 59
Suggestions, 38 39
Suing for damages, 137
Summary sheets, 112
Sunlight, 76
Suppliers, 21
Supply of Goods Acts, 142
Surveys, 124
Suspended ceilings, 4
Suspicions
  staff, 81

Takings, 111
Tatty goods, 29
Tax, 83, 116
  avoidance, 116
  evasion, 116
  reducing, 116
  retiring/selling, 116
  wages, 83
Television, 93
Temperatures
  freezer, 75, 77
  shop, 3
Temptations, 83
Theft, 107
Thieves, 89–94, 121
  quiet times, 91
Ticketing, 93, 137–139
Tickets
  pricing, 139
  more than one, 139
Tidiness, 61, 73
Till rolls, 13
Tills, 10, 84–85, 88
  checking, 84
  colour coding, 88
  discrepancies, 84
  drawers, 88
  open at night, 88
  'over', 84
Time off, 82
Tins, opening, 46
Title of goods, 140
Torts Act 1977, 141
Tourism boards, 51
Trade
  associations, 147–151
  journals, 151
  magazines, 119
Trading Standards, 11, 136

'Traffic jams', 7
Trusting roundsmen, 34

UHT treated, 44
Uncollected goods, 141
Under age, 68
Underline prices, 89
Underringing, 84
Unfair dismissal, 134
Uniforms
  school, 31
  staff, 37, 81
Unsigned cheques, 40
Unusual
  actions, 84
  transactions, 111

VAT, 16, 59, 101, 116–117, 109
  changes, 116
  inspections, 117
  retail prices, 16
  returns, 109
  schemes, 117
Vacuum packers, 19, 46–47
Valentine's Day, 28
Valuable goods, 93
Valuing a business, 122
Vandalism, 2
Vegetables, 60–63
Verbal contracts, 140

Video
  recorders, 64, 84, 93
  rental, 64–66
Voluntary associations, 146
Vulnerability, 94

Wage rates, 83
Wages, 82–83
  backdated, 83
  cash/cheques, 82
  claims, 125
  Council, 83
Wall freezers, 73
Walls, 4
Warmth, 3
Washing equipment, 6
Wastage, 29, 82
Waste containers, 7
Water meters, 12
Weather, 3
Weighing, 22
Whipping cream, 44
Wholesale licences, 69–70
Wills, 126–127
Windows, 2, 95
Wines, 70–71
Work surfaces, 52
Wrappings, 52, 61
Written statements of dismissal, 134
  contract, 131

Young males, 90
Young persons, 68